VEDIC PHYSICS

Also by the author:

India before Alexander: A New Chronology

India after Alexander: The Age of Vikramādityas

India after Vikramāditya: The Melting Pot

Vedic Physics

Scientific Origin of Hinduism

Raja Ram Mohan Roy, Ph.D.

Mount Meru Publishing

Originally published in 1999 by
Golden Egg Publishing
1245 Dupont Street, P.O. Box 99045
Toronto, Ontario, Canada M6H 4H7

This reprint of the original paperback version with minor editorial changes published in 2015 by:
Mount Meru publishing
P.O. Box 30026
Cityside Postal Outlet PO
Mississauga, Ontario
Canada L4Z 0B6
Email: mountmerupublishing@gmail.com

ISBN 978-1-988207-04-9

Vedic Physics

Scientific Origin of Hinduism

Raja Ram Mohan Roy, Ph.D.

Mount Meru Publishing

Originally published in 1999 by
Golden Egg Publishing
1245 Dupont Street, P.O. Box 99045
Toronto, Ontario, Canada M6H 4H7

This reprint of the original paperback version with minor editorial changes published in 2015 by:
Mount Meru publishing
P.O. Box 30026
Cityside Postal Outlet PO
Mississauga, Ontario
Canada L4Z 0B6
Email: mountmerupublishing@gmail.com

ISBN 978-1-988207-04-9

Dedicated to Vedic Sages

CONTENTS

FOREWORD xi
PREFACE xv
1. The Vedic Legacy 1
1.1: The Vedas 3
1.2: The Vedas and cosmology 6
1.3: The Indus Valley Civilization 7
1.4: The Avestā 8
1.5: The Brāhmaṇas 9
1.6: The Āraṇyakas and the Upaniṣads 10
1.7: The Sūtra literature 11
1.8: The Vedāṅgas, Pariśiṣṭas and Anukramaṇis 12
1.9: The Purāṇas 12
1.10: Meanings of the Vedas 13
1.11: The dating of Vedas 16
1.12: Commentators on the Vedas 18
2. The Time before Time 21
2.1: The Golden Womb 21
2.2: Water everywhere 24
2.3: Deluge that never came 25
2.4: The Creator 26
3. All this is Puruṣa 29
3.1: The Puruṣa hymn 30
3.2: Man in the image of God 38
3.3: Secret of the Unicorn 38
3.4: Puruṣa sacrifice 41
3.5: The concept of paradise 42
3.6: The Prajāpati 42
4. The Expanding Egg 45
4.1: The expanding universe 45
4.2: The birth of gods 46
4.3: The dead egg 47
4.4: The Lord of expansion 50
4.5: Puruṣa and Aditi 53
4.6: Agastya and Lopāmudra 54

5. Edge of the Universe 57
- 5.1: Indra and Vṛtra 57
- 5.2: Frog who drank all the waters 60
- 5.3: Electric force 61
- 5.4: Surface tension 62
- 5.5: Slaying of Varāha 62
- 5.6: Bubbles and voids in space 63
- 5.7: Deeds of Indra 64
- 5.8: Indra, the Bull 67
- 5.9: Mighty Hercules 68
- 5.10: Serpent as evil 68

6. Parallel Spaces 71
- 6.1: Three spaces 72
- 6.2 The steps of Viṣṇu 74
- 6.3: The hidden spaces 77

7. The Seat of Immortality 81
- 7.1: The wedding of Vivasvāna 82
- 7.2: The field 83
- 7.3: Fabric of the universe 84
- 7.4: Heaven and Earth 85
- 7.5: The cosmic tree 86
- 7.6: The giant tortoise 88
- 7.7: The geocentric universe 89
- 7.8: Superspace 90
- 7.9: Triśirā Viśvarūpa 93
- 7.10: The dark matter 95

8. Return of the Elements 97
- 8.1: Agni (Fire) 97
- 8.2: Āpaḥ (Water) 98
- 8.3: Rudra 100
- 8.4: Maruta (wind) 102
- 8.5: Saraswatī 105

9. Quark Confinement 111
- 9.1: Particle 112
- 9.2: Bosons and Fermions 113
- 9.3: Once-born and twice-born 115
- 9.4: The Flying Horse 115
- 9.5: Animal sacrifice 119
- 9.6: Quarks 121
- 9.7: The sacred cow 124

10. Matter and Energy 127
10.1: Savitā 127
10.2: Pūṣā 130
10.3: Lord of the animals 133
11. Electron, Proton and Neutron 137
11.1: Varuṇa 137
11.2: Ahuramazdā 140
11.3: Mitra 141
11.4: Rise and fall of Mithraism 143
11.5: Aryamā 146
12. Electricity and Magnetism 149
12.1: Soma 149
12.2: Indu 151
12.3: Madhu 152
12.4: Aśvins 154
13. Let There be Light 159
14. The Dance of Creation 165
14.1: Uṣā (the dawn) 165
14.2: Nakta (the night) 170
14.3: Lord of the dancers 171
15. Pair Production 173
15.1: Matter and anti-matter 173
15.2: Yama and Yamī 175
15.3: Saramā and Paṇi 179
16. The Seven Sages 183
16.1: Vasiṣṭha 184
17. The Gods Gallery 191
17.1: Three-fold division 191
17.2: Thirty three gods 192
17.3: The age of Purāṇas 193
17.4: Incarnations of Viṣṇu 194
17.5: The legend of Vikramāditya 195
18: Did Big Bang Happen? 199
18.1: The Big Bang Cosmology 200
18.2: The Steady State Cosmology 202
18.3: The singularity problem 203
18.4: The horizon problem 203
18.5: The flatness problem 204
18.6: The age problem 205
18.7: The monopole problem 206

18.8: The entropy problem 206
18.9: The antimatter problem 207
19. The Vedic Cosmology 209
19.1: The cosmic egg 209
19.2: The chakra of Viṣṇu 210
19.3: Rotation of the universe 211
19.4: The universe without singularity 213
19.5: Conservation of space, matter and energy 215
19.6: Gamma-ray bursts 215
19.7: Evolution of the universe 218
19.8: Trinity 220
19.9: The horizon Problem 220
19.10: The flatness problem 221
19.11: The age problem 222
19.12: The monopole problem 222
19.13: The entropy problem 223
19.14: The antimatter problem 223
19.15: Implications of the Vedic model 224
19.16: Cyclic cosmology 226
19.17: Vedic model and other cosmologies 228
20. The Astronomical Code 231
Scientific Glossary 235
Notes 237
Bibliography 239
Index 241

FOREWORD

The Vedic texts are a great puzzle to historians. These ancient hymns and their prose commentaries ask the most subtle questions about the nature of self, questions that the West has started asking only recently. What was the cultural context in which Vedic ideas arose? Was the mystical basis of Vedic thought connected to a comprehensive system of knowledge in which the outer sciences had their own place?

Western scholars have considered spirituality and psychology to be the main contribution of Vedic thought. That this is incorrect is clear from the recent scholarship that shows that the Vedic people knew considerable mathematics, astronomy, medicine and other sciences. The chronological frame for Indian culture has also undergone a revision. Archaeological studies have shown that there is continuity in Indian culture that goes back to about 8000 B.C. The Indian rock art has even longer prehistory; experts have claimed that the oldest paintings are about 40,000 years old.

Raja Ram Mohan Roy's book adds to this emerging picture with an audacious reinterpretation of Vedic system of knowledge. Roy's basic premise is that the mind – by analysis, reflection on every day phenomena, and grasping the nature of its own self – can discover a considerable amount of science, and this is what the Vedic rishis did. He presents a new framework for the understanding of the Vedic hymns from the point of view of physics and then he draws parallels with recent theories on the nature of the universe.

Roy's method goes counter to the orthodoxy that outer knowledge cannot be discovered by an analysis of the inner. But there is accumulating evidence from cognitive science and biology that the inner and the outer are connected. For example, biological systems are equipped with clocks tuned to the motions of the sun, the moon, and other astronomical phenomena. Indian thinkers have always insisted on the presence of such connections, claiming that this is how the mind is able to know the physical world. In Vedic thought this is expressed by the notion of "bandhu" that connect the biological, the terrestrial, and the astronomical. In that sense, Raja Roy belongs to the classical Indian tradition.

The commonly held view of science is that painstaking observations of the regularities in nature led us to the discovery of the universal laws. The process began with the planets, then it took on terrestrial phenomena, ultimately encompassing biology, genetics, and finally the current frontier of brain and mind. This process is stood on its head in the Indian texts. They speak of mind and of the nerves in the brain and connections between senses and the outer world. The madhu-vidyā of the Upaniṣads is the doctrine of the bandhu, as in honey and bees. The Puruṣa of the cosmos and that of the individual are the ātman, the immortal Brahman, the whole universe (idam sarvam). The bandhu between the large and the subtle include: earth and body; water and seed; sun and eye; moon and wind; wind and breath; fire and speech; and so on. This is to affirm that knowing oneself one can know the world!

The Vedic focus on mind and consciousness is paralleled by the central place of the observer in modern physics. In quantum mechanics the state changes in abrupt fashion when an observation is made and this has prompted some physicists to claim that consciousness should be a primary category of the universe, distinct from physical matter. Not everyone agrees. There are those who claim that consciousness emerges out of the complexity of the organization of the brain. But nobody has been able to provide a credible model of this process.

The lowly animals possess abilities of pattern discrimination that go beyond any computer. Animal intelligence appears to be a riddle and its resolution may lie in the bold ideas of the modern physicists that echo the old rishis of the Vedas. Free will cannot be squared with scientific determinism, where everything is a part of the web of stimulus and response. In this web, how can understanding arise? On the other hand, an active consciousness leaves room for freedom. It doesn't explain where and how this agency operates within the brain-machine. That such a paradox remains was known to the Vedic rishis.

I described the matter in the form of a verse once:

> Crawling the tear between being and becoming
> our exertions create vibrations
> that ease the path
> and change time past
> If the past is made of stone
> how can there be any freedom
> in our breathing?
> We make history when we observe
> the slashing of the fabric
> of time past and time future
> opens the window on freedom.
> Connections bind us
> from time to non-time
> beyond the seven sounds
> of rivers
> bells
> brazen vessels
> wheels of carriage
> croakings of frogs
> rain
> the echo in the cavern.

The Vedic hymns are full of statements that, if taken literally, make no sense. It is also full of riddles and unusual images. One needs to define a suitable context to understand why horses may have wings or the cosmic man has thousand heads, thousand eyes, and thousand feet. The tripartite model of knowledge at the basis of the hymns helps in their understanding. Roy claims we can go even further by considering specific physical associations for Vedic gods. Roy has views on the archaeology of ancient India also. He claims that the Sindhu-Saraswatī cultural tradition is the locus of the Vedic people. This claim is being increasingly made by scholars and so Roy is not alone. He uses this identity, together with his interpretive apparatus, to propose solution to several old problems related to the Harappan civilization.

But could the Vedic rishis have anticipated physics with its categories of different kinds of particles and forces? Certainly not in the direct sense that physics is described now. That the rishis did anticipate subtle notions of potential and atomic structure is known through the systems of Sāṃkhya and Vaiśeṣika. It is plausible that they had an intuitive idea of more categories, not systematized in the darśanas. Did they do so from the patterns the outer senses and the inner instrument of the mind create? And do these patterns conform to the nature of the physical universe? In other words, can we say if there is an ultimate book of physics then it can also be read by decrypting the nature of our senses?

Roy's book is a bold, new way of looking at Vedic Physics. Since he is a pioneer, this is not the place to quibble with the details of his story. We celebrate the new path he has hewn through the bush of old scholarship. It is the task of future researchers to further sharpen and modify the ideas of Roy.

Subhash Kak, Ph.D.
Author of The Astronomical Code of the Ṛgveda
Tulum, Yucatan
August 12, 1999

PREFACE

Who am I? Why am I here? These are the questions that have arisen in my mind since as long as I can remember. Perhaps it was because of the Saṃskāra I received from my father, who woke me up very early in the morning every day and recited verses from Rāmacharitamānasa, when I was a kid. I was spiritually oriented from my childhood. As a young boy, I read the Gita regularly and tried to follow its teachings. In school Mathematics and Physics were my favourite subjects. When I got an opportunity to learn Sanskrit in school, I found Sanskrit as fascinating as Mathematics and Physics.

In school and college I kept reading books on Hindu religion and philosophy to find the answers to the deepest questions of existence. In university I came across relativity and quantum mechanics, and found these subjects fascinating. Somewhere deep inside I had the feeling that I would find the answers to the quest of my existence in the discoveries of modern science. I reasoned that if religion presents the true view of the reality, then it cannot be contradictory to the findings of science. However, they presented diametrically opposite views of the same world, and it became a question of choosing which one best represents the reality. I kept on weighing the evidence, and by the time I had finished my Ph.D. in Materials Science and Engineering at a reputed university in USA, I found the evidence to be overwhelmingly in the favour of modern science. May be it was the intellectual environment of American universities, or it was my specialization, I had become a more materialistic person than I used to be, and I had become more or less an atheist. Science presented to me a world without a God, a world without any meaning and a world without any purpose for existence. This was not a very comfortable position to live by, but I was prepared to live with it, if that is what all the evidence pointed to. However, deep inside I had doubts, and questions kept on surfacing in my mind. Could modern science be wrong somewhere? After all, modern science does not explain satisfactorily how randomness can generate such complex structures as human beings. As a last attempt to find the meaning and purpose of life, I started to read the most sacred scripture of Hinduism, the Ṛgveda. It is a very difficult book to follow, with no apparent planning behind its organization. It was when I was reading the ninetieth hymn of the tenth book of the Ṛgveda, known as Puruṣa hymn that an idea struck me. This hymn is about the creation of the universe from the Supreme Being. The eighth verse talks about the creation of domesticated and wild animals. I said to myself that so far the creation story was making sense, and suddenly the subject of animals has come up. What were animals doing so early in creation? Then, I realized suddenly that it was not about animals at all. Domesticated animals live together and wild animals live alone. Domesticated animals are symbolic representation of particles that live together and wild animals are symbolic representation of particles that live alone. These particles, called bosons and fermions, are very familiar to physicists. If my reasoning was correct, then it was likely that the Vedas are a coded book. After that I started to read the Vedas very carefully, wondering about the meaning of each term I encountered. Soon, it became clear that I was not dealing with primitive intelligence here, as all the history books declare. It became clear that the Vedic sages had discovered the subtle nature of reality, and coded it in the form of the Vedas. This would explain the reason why extraordinary steps were taken to preserve the Vedas, and the honor given to the Vedas by the Hindus, even though its meaning is little understood.

One argument that is often invoked to discredit such attempts as to finding scientific meaning of scriptures, is why do these interpretations are made only after the discovery of scientific facts. I am well aware of this argument, and I have tried to show how the scientific meaning of the Vedas is very different from what modern science says. The cosmology of the Vedas is completely different from modern cosmologies, and without understanding the Vedic cosmology, the Vedas would seem meaningless. All the information that I have used to arrive at my interpretation is presented in this book. At some point the reader may start to wonder whether all these verses are really there in the scriptures. I would like to assure the reader that I have taken extreme care in providing the exact references to the sources used in this study. We are often told that the Vedas contain very abstruse scientific information, but we cannot pinpoint to specific verses in the Vedas, if we are asked to prove this point. Nothing is said in this book without providing the specific location of the verse in the scripture. The verses have been translated in English as close as possible to the apparent meaning. The scientific meaning of the verse is then explained by dissecting the words and providing supporting evidence from other scriptures. The reader is encouraged to go to the original sources in the case of doubt. I have not made up any mantras, and this can be verified easily, as Hindu scriptures are thousands of years old, and standard versions of these scriptures are easily available. All I have done is to provide a framework in which these mantras start to make sense. Once we understand that the Ṛgveda is a book of particle physics and cosmology then it becomes clear by reading the scriptures following the Vedas that this ancient science was gradually forgotten over time. It also follows that modern science is not the only way to investigate the subtle nature of reality.

I am indebted to my parents for the Saṃskāra I received from them. I would like to express my sincere appreciation to my wife Manju for her continued and enthusiastic support for this work. Professor Subhash Kak deserves a very special acknowledgement for his review, support, advice and encouragement. I would also like to thank David Frawley for reading the draft and providing critical comments and suggestions.

Raja Ram Mohan Roy
Toronto, Canada
August 28, 1998

TRANSLITERATION GUIDE

अ	a	आ	ā		
इ	i	ई	ī		
उ	u	ऊ	ū	ऋ	ṛ
ए	e	ऐ	ai		
ओ	o	औ	au		
अं	ṃ	अः	ḥ		
क	k	ख	kh		
ग	g	घ	gh	ङ	ṅ
च	ch*	छ	chh*		
ज	j	झ	jh	ञ	ñ
ट	ṭ	ठ	ṭh		
ड	ḍ	ढ	ḍh	ण	ṇ
त	t	थ	th		
द	d	ध	dh	न	n
प	p	फ	ph		
ब	b	भ	bh	म	m
य	y	र	r		
ल	l	व	v		
श	ś	ष	ṣ	स	s
ह	h	क्ष	kṣ	त्र	tr
ज्ञ	jñ	श्र	śr		

*Slightly different from International Alphabet of Sanskrit Transliteration scheme.

"In ancient and modern times, wonderful ideas have been carried forward from one race to another. It has been always with the blast of trumpets and the march of embattled cohorts. Each idea had to be soaked in a deluge of blood. ... Each word of power had to be followed by the groans of millions, by the wails of orphans, by the tears of widows. This, many other nations have taught, but India for thousands of years peacefully existed. ... Ideas after ideas have marched out from her, but every word has been spoken with a blessing behind it and peace before it. We, of all nations of the world, have never been a conquering race, and that blessing is on our head, and therefore we live."

- Swāmī Vivekānanda

1. THE VEDIC LEGACY

"Veda is the source of all Dharma" declares Manusmṛti 2.6. As we shall see this statement is no exaggeration. There is no major religion on this planet, which has not been influenced by the Vedas. The creation stories of all major religions are based on the Vedas. Though all other religions have forgotten their Vedic root or have been forgotten, there is one religion, Hinduism, which has kept the flame of the Vedic wisdom burning continuously. In order to understand Hinduism, we have to go five thousand years back in time to the region on both sides of Indo-Pakistani border, for here a mighty civilization once arose, and from the scientific achievements of these people a way of life emerged, which was later termed Hinduism. This civilization is called Indus Valley Civilization, and their scientific knowledge was coded in the sacred books called "Vedas". Veda means knowledge and is derived from root "Vida" meaning to know. The knowledge was passed from generation to generation with the explicit instructions that no matter what happened not a single letter of this body of knowledge should be changed. Great care was taken to preserve the Vedas, and we are fortunate that it has come to us in the same form it was intended.

The Vedas are the foundation of Hinduism and most authoritative of all Hindu scriptures, which are divided in two groups. First group is called Śruti meaning heard and second group is called Smṛti meaning memory. In a liberal sense, the Vedas, the Brāhmaṇas, the Āraṇyakas and the Upaniṣads are considered Śruti, while in a conservative sense only the Vedas are considered Śruti. Rest of the scriptures including the Dharma Śāstras and the Purāṇas are considered Smṛti. There are four Vedas: Ṛgveda, Yajurveda, Sāmaveda, and Atharvaveda. The Vedas are considered Apauruṣeya meaning not authored by a human being. The traditional viewpoint is that the Vedas were heard by sages during deep meditation and are the work of God. Somewhat in contrast with the viewpoint of different sages receiving the Vedic knowledge at different epochs is another traditional viewpoint that the Vedas were given to mankind in the beginning of creation by God. Here we have to make a distinction between the knowledge contained in the Vedas and when that knowledge was discovered. The electron had existed before it was discovered. As we will see in this book, the Vedas are about ancient cosmology. The laws governing the evolution of universe have existed from the beginning of the universe. This explains why the Vedas are as old as the universe. However, the viewpoint of the Vedas being received by mankind in the beginning is wrong, because there were no human beings back then. The major contention of this book is that the Vedas were discovered at the dawn of Indus Valley Civilization, and therefore the Vedas have been discovered only 5000 years ago.

1.1: The Vedas

What are the Vedas about? Are they product of primitive minds, who were expressing the natural phenomena of rain, clouds and thunder as medieval commentators describe? Are they songs of pastoral people as modern historians say? Have Hindus been wrong all along? Why did the Hindus have so much respect for a book that is seemingly about cows and horses, about rain and clouds? What is that extra-ordinary knowledge in the Vedas, so that the Indians for thousands of years have considered it as the source of all knowledge? In Manusmṛti 2.7, the Vedas are told to be the books of all fields of knowledge. In Sanskrit the word for believer is "Āstika". In other parts of the world a believer means one who believes in God. In India it was not so. Āstika meant one who believed in the Vedas. Manusmṛti 2.11 declares that "nāstiko vedanindakaḥ" meaning one who criticizes the Vedas is a non-believer. One may not believe in God and can still be a believer.

The most authoritative among the four Vedas is called Ṛgveda. Other three Vedas contain several verses that are found in the Ṛgveda also. Each verse in the Ṛgveda is set to a meter called Chhanda and has pronunciation marks called Svara. Each verse has one or more sages (Ṛṣis) and deities (Devatās) associated with it. Ṛṣis are supposed to have written or received the verse, and Devatā is supposed to be the gods in whose praise the verse has been written. Nirukta 2.11 describes Ṛṣi as one who has seen the mantras. There are big problems with this traditional viewpoint. Several of the sages as well as deities are animals or inanimate objects like fish, frog, rivers and stones. Several verses have more than one sages and deities. There is a very simple solution to this problem. The Ṛgveda is the book of ancient cosmology, where the authors have chosen fundamental particles and forces of nature to describe the cosmology in a dramatic way. Sages are not the authors of the verses, but they are also fundamental particles and forces, and so are the deities. Thus the sages Vasiṣṭha and Viśwāmitra are not sages, and deities Mitra and Varuṇa are not gods, but they all have precise scientific meaning. This viewpoint puts a constraint on each mantra. The sage and deity of the mantra must be present at the epoch described by the mantra. For example when a mantra describes what was there before the creation, sage and deity of that mantra cannot be what was not there before the creation. The Puruṣa hymn of the Ṛgveda (10.90) describes the moment of creation, and we find that sage and deity both of this hymn is God himself, because nothing else was present at that time. The scientific interpretation of the Vedas also explains why there are no hymns dedicated to Aryamā, because dedication of hymns itself has a scientific meaning. We will learn more about this when we discuss Aryamā later in this book.

A great deal of effort has gone into passing the Vedas in their original form. The Vedas were passed on orally, but it is a vast body of literature, and very minor changes crept in among the different teachers. This gave rise to different branches of the Vedas, which are nearly the same. They vary sometimes in the pronunciation of the words, or sometimes have words replaced by other words with similar meaning apparently to clear the confusion in the meaning of the verse, and in very rare cases replacement of a verse by another. Śaunaka has mentioned five branches of Ṛgveda, but currently only one of them called Śākala is available. The Yajurveda has two branches, which differ significantly from each other. One of them is called Śukla or white Yajurveda, and the other is called Kṛṣṇa or black Yajurveda. Mahīdhara in his commentary on the white Yajurveda gives a strange story about how Yajurveda became two. Vaiśampāyana taught the Yajurveda to Yājñavalkya, and once he got upset with him. So he asked Yājñavalkya to return the Yajurveda. Yājñavalkya vomited the Yajurveda by the practice of Yoga, and other students of Vaiśampāyana ate it by taking the form of birds (Tittiri). Thus the Yajurveda became black, and this branch is called the Taittirīya Saṃhitā. Yājñavalkya prayed to the sun and the sun came in the form of a horse (Vājin) to return the Yajurveda. Thus the white Yajurveda is called the Vājasaneyī Saṃhitā. What seems likely is that the Yajurveda has been written in two parts originally based on some scientific considerations. There are references to twelve branches of the black Yajurveda in the Purāṇas, out of which three are available called Taittirīya, Maitrāyaṇī and Kaṭha Saṃhitā. Seventeen branches of the white Yajurveda are mentioned, but only two are available called the Vājasaneyī or Mādhyandina Saṃhitā and the Kāṇva Saṃhitā. Normally when Yajurveda is mentioned, the Vājasaneyī branch of the white Yajurveda is meant. Three branches of the Sāmaveda are available currently, Kauthuma, Rāṇāyaṇīya and Jaiminīya, first one being the most popular. Patañjali has referred to nine branches of the Atharvaveda, but only two have survived, Paippalāda and Śaunaka, later being more popular.

The Atharvaveda has been the subject of intense discussion among scholars, many of whom do not even accept it as part of the Vedas. Some scholars even go to the extent of saying that there is only one Veda, the Ṛgveda. Whatever be the case, it is accepted by everyone that the Ṛgveda is the oldest Veda and the most authentic. This book is mostly concerned with the Ṛgveda, and shows that the Ṛgveda is a book of cosmology. I have quoted other Vedas and later scriptures in order to interpret and corroborate the meaning of the Ṛgveda. Once the physics of the Ṛgveda is completely understood, I believe that the other Vedas can be tested for their authenticity. As the Ṛgveda is a book of cosmology, it obviously follows that there is no human history in the Ṛgveda.

1.2: The Vedas and cosmology

Whether there is human history in the Vedas or not, has been a subject of controversy from the beginning. The Vedas are considered eternal and logic demands that an eternal book cannot contain mundane stories about human beings. While most commentators agreed with this view, many of them still elaborated about several Vedic themes as history. The main reason being that they hardly had any clue as to what the Vedas were about. The Vedas have been extensively studied and commented on by Indian intellectuals for all through history. Several of them certainly had the idea that the Vedas are about cosmology, but by that time the scientific means by which the Vedas were discovered and disseminated were lost. With the rise of modern science it should have been feasible to crack the Vedic code at least three decades earlier, but here lies the greatest tragedy of India. Under the Marxist grip Indian intellectuals have been made ashamed of their heritage, and most educated Hindus are ready to parade with the banner "We are ashamed to be Hindu" at the drop of a hat. Most educated Indians including scientists have no clue as to what is in the Vedas. The Vedas are written in Sanskrit and most educated Indians cannot understand it as there is a conspiracy to finish Sanskrit and everything else that Hindus should be proud of. There are very few Vedic scholars left in India. Study of the Vedas is in the state of rapid decline. The families which recite and remember the Vedas can be counted on fingers. The Vedic scholars have little knowledge of modern science, and scientists have little knowledge of the Vedas, and for this reason the real meaning of the Vedas has eluded us. Many Vedic scholars have come to the conclusion that the Vedas are primarily concerned with cosmology, however they are not in a position to show that the Vedic cosmology has the solutions to the most difficult problems of modern cosmology. Yudhiṣṭhira Mīmāṃsaka writes [1]:

"From the study of the Vedic literature several times I have come to the conclusion that Śrauta Yajñas are only a representation of the evolution of universe from its beginning to the end. Like dramas are played to remember history, the process of various Śrauta Yajñas describes the science of cosmology."

He could not have said it better, but the problem is that the Vedic scholars and modern scientists have never sat together to discover the ultimate secret of the cosmos.

1.3: The Indus Valley Civilization and the Mahābhārata war

The knowledge contained in the Vedas is very abstruse, and is well beyond the comprehension of ordinary human beings. Therefore Vedic sages coded the knowledge in a simple form in which it could be understood by everyone. The Ṛgveda itself testifies that it has a hidden meaning in verse 4.3.16. Sage Bharata in his Nāṭyaśāstra 1.23 refers to sages who knew the hidden meaning of the Vedas. This coding of knowledge proved to be very successful in disseminating the knowledge to common folks, which is evident from the seals found in Indus Valley Civilization. Almost all the seals have Vedic motif and the writings also represent Vedic ideas. The people of Indus Valley Civilization seem preoccupied with the Vedic knowledge, which is only understandable considering that they possessed the scientific knowledge from which even modern scientists can learn. For nearly thousand years there was little change in the life of the Vedic people. There must have been scientific ways through which this knowledge was obtained. On the eve of "Mahābhārata war" our ancestors believed that their knowledge was in the danger of being lost. They anticipated the disaster that was coming, and deliberated about how to save the Vedic knowledge. They could have written it down, but writings could be destroyed. Therefore they decided that they will organize the Vedic knowledge and instruct pupils to memorize it, who will pass it on orally. The chief Vedic scientist was Kṛṣṇa Dvaipāyana also known as Vedavyāsa, who taught the Ṛgveda to Paila, the Sāmaveda to Jaimini, the Yajurveda to Vaiśampāyana and the Atharvaveda to Sumantu (Bhāgavata 1.4.21). They taught it to other pupils and they in turn to more other pupils. These pupils spread in every direction and tried to conserve the Vedas from disappearing.

1.4: The Avestā

One group reached Iran and started to practice Vedic Dharma there. The religious scripture of ancient Iranians was the Avestā. The Avestā available today is only a fraction of what existed thousands of years ago. When Alexander captured Iran before 326 B. C. after a bloody war, he destroyed each copy of the Avestā available. After return of political stability Persian priests tried to salvage the Avestā and much was written out of memory. But bad luck returned again to Persians in the seventh century when they were defeated by Muslim invaders in 642 A.D. Within a hundred years Persians were forcibly converted to Islam. Few Persians fled Persia in search of a place where they could freely worship and follow their religion. They returned to their original homeland in India where they are a thriving community called Pārasis. The Avestā is divided in five parts: (1) Yasna, of which Gāthā is a part, (2) Vispaređā, (3) Vendidāda, (4) Yaśta, and (5) Khurdā Avestā. The Avestā can also be divided in two parts: main Avestā and Khurdā Avestā. Main Avestā includes Yasna, Vispaređā, Vendidāda, and Yaśta. There is remarkable similarity between the language of the Vedas and the Gāthā. Several words are common or there is a difference of one letter. Grammar and meters are also similar.

1.5: The Brāhmaṇas

After Mahābhārata war the knowledge contained in the Vedas was gradually lost. As the knowledge contained in the Vedas started to make no sense at all, it became difficult to preserve the knowledge. To preserve the meaning of the Vedas, commentaries on the Vedas were written. These are called the Brāhmaṇas, and the most comprehensive of them is the Śatapatha Brāhmaṇa. To preserve the structure of Vedas, Prātiśākhya books, Sikṣā books and Anukramaṇikā books were written.

All Brāhmaṇas are associated with a Veda. The Aitareya Brāhmaṇa and the Kauṣītaki Brāhmaṇa are associated with the Ṛgveda. The Brāhmaṇa of the Taittirīya branch of the black Yajurveda is the Taittirīya Brāhmaṇa. The Śatapatha Brāhmaṇa is the Brāhmaṇa of the white Yajurveda. The Jaiminīya Brāhmaṇa is the major Brāhmaṇa related to the Sāmaveda, minor Brāhmaṇas being Sāmavidhāna, Devatādhyayī, Vaṃśa and Saṃhitopaniṣada Brāhmaṇas. The Gopatha Brāhmaṇa is related to the Atharvaveda.

The Śatapatha Brāhmaṇa is a milestone in the development of the Vedic literature. Several centuries must have passed between the Mahābhārata war and the writing of the Śatapatha Brāhmaṇa, because the Śatapatha Brāhmaṇas shows a significant loss of the Vedic science. There are several new ideas in the Śatapatha Brāhmaṇa that are not present in the Vedas. There is hardly any legend of creation among the ancient world, the seed of which cannot be shown to be in the Śatapatha Brāhmaṇa. The Second wave of emigration from India happened after the composition of the Śatapatha Brāhmaṇa, and a prominent group among them settled in Greece. The Greek mythology is a direct borrowing from the Śatapatha Brāhmaṇa. Many of the Greek legends are not found in the Vedas, but found in the Śatapatha Brāhmaṇa, and this fact puts a big hole in the theory of the original homeland being other than India. If all Indo-Europeans races had some other homeland from which they dispersed, then Greek legends should match the Vedas and not the Śatapatha Brāhmaṇa. The contention of this book is that India is the cradle of civilization, and at least three major emigrations from India have taken place at different epochs, first after the Mahābhārata war, second after the composition of the Śatapatha Brāhmaṇa and third after the composition of the early Purāṇas. The Gods are same in the Vedas and the Brāhmaṇas. A new god Prajāpati comes in the picture in the Brāhmaṇas. All gods are described as born from Prajāpati.

1.6: The Āraṇyakas and the Upaniṣads

Āraṇyaka means pertaining to forest and Upaniṣad means to sit near. Similar to the Brāhmaṇas, the Āraṇyakas and the Upaniṣads are also related to the Vedas. The Aitareya and the Śāṅkhāyana Āraṇyakas are connected to the Ṛgveda, the Tavalkāra and the Chhāndogya Āraṇyakas to the Sāmaveda, the Taittirīya and the Maitrāyaṇī Āraṇyakas to the black Yajurveda and the Bṛhadāraṇyaka to white Yajurveda. The Aitareya and the Kauṣītaki Upaniṣads are related to the Ṛgveda, the Chāndogya Upaniṣad and the Kenopaniṣada to the Sāmaveda, the Kaṭhopaniṣada, Taittirīya, Maitrī and Śvetāśvatara Upaniṣads to the black Yajurveda, the Bṛhadāraṇyaka and Īśa Upaniṣads to the white Yajurveda, and the Muṇdaka, Māṇḍūkya and Praśna Upaniṣads to the Atharvaveda. Note that the Brāhmaṇas and Upaniṣads both are based on Vedas, and therefore Upaniṣads are not product of rebellion from the ritualism of the Brāhmaṇas. The Upaniṣads contain most beautiful expressions of human thought. In Taittirīya Upaniṣad 1.11 a teacher gives the following advice to new graduates:

"Speak only the truth, follow the Dharma and don't be heedless about self-study. Mother is god, father is god, teacher is god, and guest is god. Only perform those actions which are blameless, nothing else. Follow only those of our behavior, which are good, not the others."

1.7: The Sūtra literature

The Sūtra period is considered later than the Brāhmaṇa period. The style of the Sutras is completely opposite of the Brāhmaṇas. While the Brāhmaṇas are very elaborate in their treatment of any subject, the Sūtras take recourse to extreme brevity. The Sūtra literature is of three types: Kalpasūtra or Śrautasūtra, Gṛhyasūtra and Dharmasūtra.

The Śāṅkhāyana and Āśwalāyana Śrautasūtras are related to the Ṛgveda, Masaka, Lāṭyāyana and Drāhyāyana Śrautasūtra to the Sāmaveda, the Kātyāyana Śrautasūtra is related to the white Yajurveda, Āpastamba, Hiraṇyakeśina and Baudhāyana Śrautasūtra to the black Yajurveda, and the Vaitāna Śrautasūtra to the Atharvaveda. The Śrautasūtras describe the rituals related to the Yajñas.

The Śāṅkhāyana and Āśwalāyana Gṛhyasūtras are connected to the Ṛgveda, the Gobhila Gṛhyasūtra to the Sāmaveda, the Pāraskara Gṛhyasūtra to the white Yajurveda, the Āpastamba Gṛhyasūtra to the black Yajurveda, and the Kauśika Gṛhyasūtra to the Atharvaveda. The Gṛhyasūtras describe the rituals to be performed from birth to death for a Hindu.

The Dharmasūtras are not specifically related to individual Vedas. The Dharmasūtras of Āpastamba, Hiraṇyakeśina and Baudhāyana are presently available. The Dharmasūtras discuss the behavior of the Hindus in their day-to-day life.

1.8: The Vedāṅgas, Pariśiṣṭas and Anukramaṇis

Vedāṅga means the limb of the Vedas and Pariśiṣṭa means an appendix. The Vedāṅgas are considered very important to study the Vedas. There are six Vedāṅgas: Śikṣā (Pronunciation), Chhanda (Meter), Vyākaraṇa (Grammar), Nirukta (Etymology), Jyotiṣa (Astronomy) and Kalpa (Ceremonial). The Śikṣā texts are the Prātiśākhyas of the Ṛgveda, Yajurveda and Atharvaveda. Pariśiṣṭa means appendix, and the Pariśiṣṭas explain the meaning of the Sūtras. Presently available Pariśiṣṭas are Āśwalāyanagṛhyapariśiṣṭa, Gobhila Saṃgraha Pariśiṣṭa and Chāndogyagṛhya Pariśiṣṭa. Anukramaṇis list the order of verses and other information related to the organization of the Vedas.

1.9: The Purāṇas

The Purāṇas are the latest among the Hindu scriptures. What is present as a seed in the Vedas, takes the form of a big tree in the Purāṇas. There are eighteen major Purāṇas, which are called the Mahāpurāṇas. There are eighteen minor Purāṇas called the Upapurāṇas. The Purāṇas are voluminous. The Śrīmadbhāgvata Mahāpurāṇa consists of eighteen thousand verses. The Purāṇas deal with five subjects: Sarga (creation of the universe), Pratisarga (dissolution of the universe), Vaṃśa (lineage), Manvantara (epochs), and Vaṃśānucharita (history). Most Hindus get their knowledge of Hinduism from the Purāṇas, which represent the popular form of Hinduism.

From the Vedas to the Purāṇas we have a complete record of the development of the Hindu society. The Vedas provide the solid foundation on which the magnificent palace of Hinduism has been erected. However, the Vedas are so far removed from us, that we have only retained a memory of the Vedas providing our foundation and have completely forgotten what the Vedas really represent.

1.10: Meanings of the Vedas

The Ṛgveda on the face of it seems to be a book about cows, horses and other mundane matters without any kind of organization. Why will such a book be considered the book of all knowledge since time immemorial? Only explanation is that the Ṛgveda has a hidden meaning. The Ṛgveda clearly mentions that it has a secret meaning in the following verse:

"The Vedic mantras are in the never-decaying remotest sky, where all the gods reside. One who does not know that, what will he do with Vedic mantras? One who knows that, the gods stay with him." Ṛgveda 1.164.39

The hidden names of the gods are also mentioned in Ṛgveda 1.164.5, 5.3.2, 5.3.3, 5.5.10, and 9.95.2. Thus it has always been understood that the Ṛgveda has a meaning very different from its apparent meaning. As the loss of the Vedic science continued after the period of the Brāhmaṇas, new meanings were given to the Vedas. There were two possibilities, either mantras could be altered to provide the new meaning or new meaning could be given to the words occurring in mantras. Fortunately, mantras were not altered, rather commentators wrote volumes about what each word in each mantra meant. As there was no standard for doing this exercise, some words came to mean a multitude of things. For example the word "Gau" which means cow came to have 47 different meanings including rays of sun and milk. Ahi which means serpent is often translated as cloud. Mitra, Varuṇa, Savitā, Āditya, and Indra, all came to mean the sun, even though they have completely different meaning in the Ṛgveda. Indra is often described in Ṛgveda as the one who created and placed the sun in the heaven, still he was later identified with the sun. As each word came to mean a multitude of things, any mantra could now be given hundreds of meaning. There are several translations of the

Vedas available currently, and one finds that for the same verse the translations are as different as possible.

If we think about it, there is clearly a paradox here. The Vedas are supposed to be so carefully compiled that even changing a letter was not allowed for thousands of years for the fear that its meaning will be lost, and on the other hand we are led to believe that our revered sages were so careless that they could not even use proper words. Why would the Vedic sages use the word for cow when they meant a ray of light and the word for serpent when they meant cloud? In fact each word is very carefully thought and means exactly what it says. It is not the Vedic sage who declared that "Gau" means solar ray, but later day commentators, who had forgotten the meaning of the mantras. In this book, we are going to discover an incredibly simpler picture. We will reduce the meaning of the Vedic mantras to exactly two: One what it literally says, that is the apparent meaning and other the scientific interpretation, which is the actual meaning. I will be quoting the Vedic mantras very liberally. Often, I will be translating complete hymns. I have done so for several reasons. For one, I don't want to prove my point by selective quotation. Second, most educated Indians are very ignorant of what is in the Ṛgveda. This is a nice place to know a little bit about the most sacred book of the Hindus and the first book of human race. Third and most important, what I have discovered is only the tip of the iceberg. I expect my learned readers to contribute in discovering the true meaning of the Vedas, and it is very important that I give my readers as much information as possible. The translation of the Vedic mantras in this book follows a very simple rule. I have tried to translate the mantras as close as possible to the apparent meaning, and then I have tried to explain its actual meaning. Thus I have translated Savitā as Savitā, Indra as Indra, Sūrya as Sūrya, Ahi as serpent, Gau as cow and so on. This is the most important point in rediscovering the Vedas.

Unless the reader knows the exact meaning of the mantras, the scientific meaning will elude the reader. For example a verse from Ṛgveda says the following:

"Indra created cows from serpent for Trita." Ṛgveda 10.48.2

Sātavalekara [2] translates it as "Indra created waters from cloud for Trita." This mantra does not make any sense unless the real meanings of cows and serpent are known, and therefore Gau (cow) received an additional meaning of water, and Ahi (serpent) received an additional meaning of cloud. In this book I will discuss the real meaning of Gau and Ahi, and then a great cosmic secret will be revealed by this mantra. Most translations of the Vedas differ from each other, because the translator is trying to put meaning in the mantras that are simply not there. The translations in this book are based on my own reading of mantras in Sanskrit, and a number of books on the Vedas [2-7].

When actual meaning of the Vedas was forgotten, and several meanings were imposed on each word of the Vedas, it became easy to give a lot of meaning to the Vedas that was simply not intended. As none of these meanings justified the honor given to the Vedas, scholars started to believe that there were still more meanings hidden in the Vedas, and finally a tradition started that the Vedas contain all the knowledge that is there to acquire. This viewpoint is certainly wrong, as the Vedas have a certain number of mantras, and there is only a certain number of ways it can be interpreted. When new interpretations were given to the knowledge, most of the Vedas were explained as describing natural phenomena involving sun, cloud and rain. The cosmology of the Vedas was completely forgotten, and the fundamental particles and forces of nature were deified. The interaction of particles and forces was transformed into human history that went millions of years back in time. In the confusion that was created, it became easy for ideologically motivated historians to deny the Hindus the most glorious epoch of Hinduism. Today the Vedas have returned in their pristine glory to clear all confusion, and establish the reign of truth. One major problem in ascertaining the truth is to know when the Vedas were composed.

1.11: The dating of Vedas

Tradition believes that the Vedas are as old as the universe itself, and many Vedic scholars still try to adhere to this position. This viewpoint is clearly wrong, and arises from the confusion between when the Vedas were written and what is in the Vedas. The knowledge contained in the Vedas is as old as the universe because the Vedas are about the evolution of the universe, while Vedas have been discovered only very recently. The Vedas do not give any clue as to when they were written, so scholars have resorted to other methods in determining the age of the Vedas.

One of the most illogical methods was adopted by Max Müler, famous Vedic scholar of last century, and regrettably it is the most popular up till now. Max Müler believed in the Biblical creation, and calculated the age of the Vedas as follows [8]. He assumed the creation to have taken place on October 23, 4004 B.C., and then using the biblical chronology the deluge is placed in the year 2448 B.C. He granted a thousand years for the floods to subside, thus arriving at 1400 B.C. for the Aryan invasion of India. He allowed 200 years as the time to get familiar with the new home, thus calculating 1200 B.C. as the date for the composition of the Vedas. Of course he did not provide this reasoning for his dating of the Vedas to general public, but worked backwards to give the same chronology he had already calculated. He fixed 600 B.C. for the date of Buddha, allotted 200 years each for the Chhandas, Mantra and Brāhmaṇa periods. Thus Brāhmaṇas were composed during 800-600 B.C., Mantra portion of the Vedas was composed during 1000-800 B.C. and Chhandas portion of the Vedas (e.g. Ṛgveda) was composed during 1200-1000 B.C. Obviously there is no scientific reason as to why it should take only 200 years each and not 500 or 1000 years for the composition of the Chhandas, Mantras and Brāhmaṇas. Later Max Müler disowned his chronology and said that no power on earth can determine when the Vedas were written.

Tilak and Jacobi resorted to astronomical dating of the Vedas. They interpreted few verses of the Ṛgveda to come to the conclusion that these verses describe the time period of 4500 B.C. This method is also highly questionable. There is no indication in the Ṛgveda to suggest that it is a book of astronomy, and the few verses that have been interpreted to contain astronomical information are highly mystical. The astronomical information is arrived by assuming meanings of the words very different from the apparent meanings, and remains entirely unconvincing. For example in his book Orion, Tilak interprets Ṛbhus to mean seasons, Vasta (he-goat) to mean sun and hound to mean Canis Major in Ṛgveda 1.161.3. These meanings can only be considered to be imposed on the verse. Tilak uses a verse from Gitā in which Lord Kṛṣṇa says that he is Mārgśīrṣa among the months and spring among the seasons. Tilak considers this verse to contain the memory of those days when Mārgśīrṣa used to fall during spring about 10,000 years ago. Again this is not a logical argument. The two statements about months and seasons are completely independent and there is no reason to see a connection there. Thus astronomical dating of the Vedas stands on very shaky grounds.

Some other scholars have tried to prove the antiquity of the Vedas by performing geological dating. Ṛgveda 10.136.5 talks about seas in the east and west, which cannot be applied to the area where the Vedas are supposed to have been composed. A. C. Das in his book Ṛgvedic India [9] takes the antiquity of the Vedas to beyond 25,000 years in order to justify the verses like this. As the reader will see in this book, the Ṛgveda is a coded book, and the rivers, mountains and seas of the Ṛgveda do not refer to these objects at all. Thus geological dating of the Vedas is a futile exercise.

How are we then to know about the time when the Vedas were composed? Fortunately there is a very simple way of dating the Vedas. We should remember that the Vedas did not exist by themselves, but the book that is considered so sacred in India, must have been lived by the people. Their lifestyle and belief system will show a clear mark of the Vedas. If we could find those people, then we will know the date of the Vedas. Hinduism is a dynamic religion, which has changed its form with the passage of time. We can date our scriptures by matching them with the archaeological artifacts. As I tried to do this exercise for the Ṛgveda, I found a striking match with the Indus Valley Civilization. This is only to be expected. The Ṛgveda is the oldest of our scriptures and the Indus Valley Civilization is the oldest age of the Indian civilization. Therefore it is no surprise that they match each other. We will see in this book that the Indus Valley seals represent Vedic ideas, thus proving without doubt that this civilization was the Vedic civilization and the Ṛgveda was written at the beginning of this civilization. This gives a date of 3000 B. C. for the composition of the Ṛgveda.

1.12: Commentators on the Vedas

First commentator on the Vedas is Yāska. By his time scientific meaning of the Vedas was mostly lost, and many Hindus were looking at the Vedas with suspicion. Atheist Chārvākas considered the Vedas inane and meaningless. Yāska describes the criticisms by Kautsa in Nirukta 1.15. Kautsa claimed that the Vedas are meaningless, because neither the order of words can be changed nor a word can be replaced with another word of same meaning. Kautsa also gave the example of the dialogue with inanimate objects, and said that this could be composed by mentally ill people only. He considered the Vedas meaningless also because several mantras contradict each other, like sometimes one Rudra is mentioned and sometimes thousand Rudras are mentioned. These criticisms are valid when actual meaning of the Vedas is not known. We are indeed fortunate that the Vedas have still come to us as intended, and the contribution of the Brāhmaṇas in preserving the Vedas cannot be underestimated. The Brāhmaṇas were supposed to protect the Vedas, and they have performed their job very well. Most famous commentator on the Vedas is Sāyaṇa. His commentary has been the basis for western scholars of the Vedas. Uvvaṭa and Mahīdhara have also written commentaries on the Vedas. Prominent commentators among western scholars are Roth and Max Müler. Among recent Indian scholars, the commentaries of Dayānanda, Aurobindo and Sātavalekara are prominent. Dayānanda considered the Vedas to be the books of all fields of knowledge, and he has written his commentaries to prove this point. Aurobindo has given a psychological interpretation of the Vedas. Sātavalekara follows the line of thinking of Dayānanda to certain extent. Despite all these attempts, the meaning of the Vedas has eluded mankind so far, because none of them have shown the existence of an extra-ordinary knowledge in the Vedas, which will justify the honor given to the Vedas since their discovery. This book is the first serious attempt in decoding that extra-ordinary meaning of the Vedas, and once the reader has finished this book, the reader will know the reason for the failure of earlier commentators. The physics that the Vedas talk about has not been discovered yet, and it is only now that modern physics has given humanity a foundation to launch an attempt to understand the Vedas. In fact knowledge of the Vedas was targeted for us, for what purpose, I do not know. It is a gift to humanity from the ancestors of antiquity, who have been maligned as invaders and barbarians, but they had only love for their descendents, and the Vedas are the testimony of that love.

The Vedas have guided Indian civilization for last five thousand years. The Vedas are the pillars of Hinduism. Hinduism has evolved from Vedas, but the current popular form of Hinduism is very different from that in the Vedic period. Most Hindus know about Hinduism from popular epics Rāmāyaṇa and Mahābhārata, and from Purāṇas. Hinduism has changed in form so much from the Vedic period that modern historians have argued about Indus Valley Civilization being non-Hindu, and educated Hindus have accepted it. In fact, there is simply nothing in the Indus Valley Civilization that is not part of Hinduism. The people of Indus Valley Civilization were representing the knowledge of the Vedas in various forms. Vedas formed the very basis of that civilization, which the Vedic people are accused of destroying. This accusation could gain ground, because the physics of the Vedas was completely forgotten. In this book, we will discover the lost physics of the Vedas after thousands of years, and start the process for the interpretation of so-far undeciphered Indus Valley seals.

"I cannot deny the feeling of unreality in writing about the first three minutes as if we really know what we are talking about."
- Steven Weinberg

2. THE TIME BEFORE TIME

You are about to set forth on a journey like the one you have never taken before. You are about to see things that you have never even suspected to exist. You are about to confront the wisdom from beyond. Your journey into the fascinating realm of Vedic wisdom will take you billions of years in past to a time when even time did not exist.

2.1: The Golden Womb

Imagine yourself going backward in time all the way to the first moment, when universe came into existence with the expansion of the universe. What was there before this moment of creation?

"Before creation there existed a golden womb, he was the only lord of everything born. He holds earth and this heaven." Ṛgveda 10.121.1

The creation is only a manifestation of the Supreme Being. Before creation the Supreme Being existed in an unmanifested form. This form is called a golden womb, a womb because the whole universe originated from it. Why the womb is considered golden? Gold has a special color. Materials turn golden at very high temperature. The womb from which sun, stars and galaxies are formed, golden is an appropriate adjective for that. Gold is thus the color of energy in the Vedic literature. The association of gods with gold in Hindu Dharma is a symbolic representation of gods being various forms of energy. The idols of gods have always been adorned by gold for this reason, and this is the reason for the excessive attachment of Hindus with gold. At one time India was called the golden sparrow, because Indians had accumulated vast quantities of gold during thousands of years of civilization and it was the richest country in the world. The legends of its riches were spread in faraway places, and voyagers were so fascinated with India that wherever they landed, they called the native inhabitants Indians. The state of being before the creation is described with precision in the Nāsdīya hymn of the Ṛgveda.

Ṛgveda 10.129

Sage: Prajāpati Parameṣṭhī; Deity: Bhāvavṛtta; Meter: Triṣṭupa

1. There was neither manifested nor unmanifested. Then there was no dust and there was no sky beyond that. What was covering, where was whose shelter? What was the deep, inexplicable sound?

2. There was neither death nor immortality. There was no differentiation between night and day. Only he was there by his own will without air. There was nothing beyond him.

3. Earlier there was darkness, everything was enveloped in darkness. All this was undifferentiated fluid (Salila). Whatever was, was covered in emptiness. That one was born from heat.

4. Earlier (before creation) desire (to create) arose in him. Then from his mind first seed was born. Wise men by reasoning found the manifested bonded to unmanifested.

5. Its rays spread oblique, down and up. He became the begetter. He became great by his own will below and beyond.

6. Who knows, who will tell here that from where and why this creation was born, because gods were born after the moment of creation. Therefore, who knows from whom this was born?

7. From whom this creation was born, he upholds this or not. Its lord who resides in the remotest sky, may be he knows or may be even he does not.

The state of being before the creation was way beyond we can comprehend by senses. There was emptiness, and everything we can observe was not there. There was neither space nor time. There was neither matter nor energy. This is a very important concept in Vedic cosmology. Modern physics tells us that all the matter and energy was concentrated in a point, while verses one to three clearly emphasize that the Vedas consider universe to be completely empty in the beginning. The Taittirīya Brāhmaṇa says:

"Earlier there was absolutely nothing. There was no heaven, no earth and no atmosphere." Taittirīya Brāhmaṇa 2.2.9.1

This has very important consequence for the evolution of the universe as we will see. Modern physics tells us that the universe started infinitely hot, which cooled down rapidly with the expansion of the universe. The Vedas tell us the opposite. The universe was extremely cold in the beginning. The evolution of the universe started with the rise in temperature. In verse three, the cause of universe is said to be tapa. Tapa is a very important concept in Hinduism. In post-Vedic Hinduism, Tapa comes to mean the performance of austerity in deep forests, the result of which could be the gain of immense power. Tapa means to heat, to warm up, and it is in this sense that tapa is used in the Vedas. The evolution of universe started with the creation of matter, energy and space, the effect of which was to warm up the universe. In this way the whole universe could be considered to be born out of Tapa.

2.2: Water everywhere

There was complete darkness earlier and all that existed was Salila (Ṛgveda 10.129.3 quoted above). Salila means water, but in the Ṛgveda it is a technical term which means undifferentiated primordial fluid. In the verse Salila is preceded by the adjective "apraketa" meaning undifferentiated, which leaves no doubt about its intended meaning. The Ṛgveda is a book of ancient cosmology, which uses common words known to the Indus Valley people, so that everyone could understand the most abstruse concepts. For us, who are far removed in time from those people, the Vedas are the only guide to understand their way of life. This is not an easy task, because the real meaning of the Vedas is very different from the apparent meaning. We have to pick up each word, try to decipher its meaning, and then see whether it fits in the framework of the Vedas. That "Salila" is a technical word in the Vedas is clearly confirmed by a mantra from the Śatapatha Brāhmaṇa. Mantra 11.1.6.1 says that Āpaḥ were indeed Salila earlier. Now Āpaḥ and Salila both mean water. If water is the intended meaning then this verse will make no sense at all. Clearly both Āpaḥ and Salila are technical terms, and cannot be used interchangeably. We can think of the words "speed" and "velocity" which in the ordinary usage are equivalent, but in physics their meanings are very different, one being a scalar quantity and the other a vector. Salila is the primordial state of the universe, when there is nothing manifest.

There is complete equilibrium and homogeneity. When this equilibrium is broken due to the action of the fundamental forces of nature, inhomogeneity is created, and this inhomogeneous state is termed Āpaḥ.

The Vedas tell us that in the beginning everything was Salila, whose apparent meaning is that there was water everywhere. This concept of water being everywhere was spread all over the world and was later borrowed by other religions. The Bible (Genesis 1.1-2 and 1.6-7) says that in the beginning the universe consisted of water only. A description of the myths of Quiches, the native Indians of South America, is found in Popol Vuh. Quiches believed that in the beginning there was nothing but water and the feathered serpent [1]. The message of Vedas was spread far and away, and the Vedic science had given rise to many popular myths.

2.3: Deluge that never came

Another widespread belief of the ancient world is that of a deluge. It is really strange that the whole world believed in such a deluge, when such a deluge had not come during the last ten thousand years. How could humans have a memory of a deluge that must have come before ten millennia if at all, while the history of civilization is of a more recent origin? Only logical answer is that it is part of a popular myth confused with reality. The cause of this confusion is the use of words Salila and Āpaḥ in the Vedic science. The Vedas use Salila to denote the primordial undifferentiated fluid, the confusion of which with water gave rise to the story of watery origins. Āpaḥ denotes the inhomogeneous state of universe. Āpaḥ also means water, and this water formed the basis of deluge stories.

The story of deluge is not found in Vedas. The oldest version of deluge is found in the Śatapatha Brāhmaṇa 1.8.1.1-6. One day Manu, son of Vivasvāna held a little water to clean his mouth. One very small fish was caught in his hand. The fish said that nourish me and I will protect you. Manu asked how the fish will protect him? The Fish said that in a few days a deluge will destroy everything and it would protect him from that. Manu asked how he could protect the fish. Fish said that put it in a pot, then in a pit, and then in sea. The fish told Manu the time of the deluge and to be ready with a boat. When the flood came, Manu rode in the boat. The fish came to him as a huge fish with one horn. Manu tied the boat with a rope to the horn of the fish. The fish took him to a mountain, and told to stay there till the flood subsided. This story transforms in the incarnation of Lord Viṣṇu as a fish in the Purāṇas.

Myth of such a deluge was prevalent among the tribes of North American Indians as well. George Catlin, a nineteenth century traveler, who lived among native Indians, tells us about the deluge myth among a tribe near west bank of Missouri in USA [2]. The Mandans believed that the human race was destroyed by the rising of the waters. Only one man survived the deluge, who landed his big canoe on a high mountain. All human beings have descended from that man. Peruvians also believed in a deluge myth [3]. Only one man and a woman survived the deluge. They floated in a box to a place several hundred miles from Cuzco. They settled there on the order of the creator. The Bible tells the story of deluge in Genesis 6.1-8.22. The cosmology of Semitic religions is a direct borrowing from Vedas.

2.4: The Creator

Verse 10.129.4 tells us that the universe was created by the desire of the Supreme Being. This is in complete contrast with modern physics. Modern science tells us that the evolution of the universe is a random phenomenon. It does not tell us why an infinitely complex structure like human being has evolved, because randomness can only increase the disorder in the universe.

Verse 10.129.5 tells that once the process of creation began, Supreme Being became great, meaning universe started to expand. In the Vedas the universe is not considered different from the Supreme Being. Expansion of the universe is a key feature of the Vedic cosmology and is in agreement with modern science, but there are very significant differences as well, and the aim of this book is to highlight those differences. A common complain, and valid as well, against scientific interpretation of the Hindu scriptures is that why do these interpretations come up only after the discovery of the scientific facts. Is there anything in the scriptures, which can be told before its scientific discovery? In this book I am going to do exactly that. At every stage I will highlight the differences, and these differences are not minute by any stretch of imagination, and then leave it to scientists to prove that the Ṛgveda is wrong. If the Ṛgveda is a product of primitive people engaged in agriculture and husbandry, then it should not take even minutes to prove that this scientific interpretation is wrong. In fact, a book detailing the science of those ancient people cannot even be attempted. One can also say that this whole science is the product of the author, and that it does not exist in the Vedas. To refute this claim, I will quote extensively from the scriptures, pick up the words from the mantras, and dissect those words to reveal the meaning behind. Soon it will become clear that we are not dealing with primitive minds, but minds that had the capability to look inside atoms on one hand, and to observe the boundaries of the universe on the other hand.

Verse 10.129.7 states that the Supreme Being resides in "Parama Vyoma." Vyoma means sky or space, and parama means remotest. Thus Supreme Being exists beyond our senses of space and time, and this is the state about which wise sages talk about during the moments of realization of truth. It will seem paradoxical, that on one hand the Vedas will not consider Supreme Being different from the universe, and still talk about him as being beyond our senses. This is so because what we normally observe is only the manifestation at a gross scale, while the ultimate realization of this concept can only occur at a very subtle scale well beyond our scientific capabilities. Let's then proceed to see in more detail what the Ṛgveda tells about the Supreme Being in the most important hymn of the Vedas, the Puruṣa hymn.

"I dwell within all beings as the soul, the pure consciousness, the ground of all phenomena, internal and external. I am both the enjoyer and that which is enjoyed. In the days of my ignorance, I used to think of these as being separate from myself. Now I know that I am all."

- Śaṅkarāchārya

3. ALL THIS IS PURUṢA

The Puruṣa hymn is considered the most important hymn in the Ṛgveda. The Importance of the Puruṣa hymn is obvious from the fact that this is the only hymn available in all four Vedas. Vedavyāsa has said in Mahābhārata, Śānti Parva, 338.5 that the Puruṣa hymn is the most important hymn in the Vedas. This is a very important point to remember that while the Indian tradition considers the Puruṣa hymn to be the most important hymn, the western scholarship considers the Puruṣa hymn to represent a savage myth. The western scholarship thus concludes that the Puruṣa hymn is a very old hymn in the Vedas, while the Nāsadīya hymn, which is very profound, is considered to be of a very late origin. We will soon see the absurdity of this viewpoint. Remember, India can be understood only from an Indian point of view, because it has a unique history. The Puruṣa hymn is the key to understanding the Vedas. In the Ṛgveda, the Puruṣa hymn consists of 16 verses, in other Vedas it consists of up to 22 verses.

In the Ṛgveda, "Puruṣa" word is used fourteen times, out of which nine times it has been used in the Puruṣa hymn itself. Puruṣa means man, but this is not the intended meaning in the Vedas. To understand the meaning of the Vedas, we have to find the etymological meaning of each word in the Vedas. Puruṣa etymologically means one who is pervading the town (Pura) or one who is sleeping in town. Pura itself means one which guards and nourishes. Here it is important to note that Pura is no ordinary town. The whole cosmos is considered the town, and the Supreme Being who pervades the cosmos is Puruṣa. Thus Puruṣa in the Vedas stands for God and this is the way Puruṣa has been described in all scriptures and commentaries following the Vedas. Śatapatha Brāhmaṇa 7.4.1.15 and Jaiminīya Brāhmaṇa 2.47 equate Puruṣa with creator Prajāpati. As this is the most important hymn of the Vedas, we will follow each verse of the Puruṣa hymn of the Ṛgveda in order to understand the meaning of the Vedas and the seals belonging to the Indus Valley Civilization.

3.1: The Puruṣa hymn

Ṛgveda 10.90

Sage: Nārāyaṇa; Deity: Puruṣa; Meter: Anuṣṭupa, 16 – Triṣṭupa

"Puruṣa has thousand heads, thousand eyes and thousand legs. He is covering Bhūmi from all around, and is beyond also in ten-finger form." Ṛgveda 10.90.1

Bhūmi means land and here it is used to denote the universe. Thousand is used in the sense of infinite. The most crucial point in this verse is that Puruṣa exists outside the universe in ten-finger form. Vedas are full of numbers like three, seven, and ten. A careful reading of the Vedas will reveal that these numbers do not occur at random as will be the case if the Vedas were poetry of pastoral people. There is a consistency about these numbers. What could ten-finger form represent? Could it represent ten-dimensions? Yāska says that directions are hand of nature in Nirukta 1.7. Taittirīya Saṃhitā 4.7.9.1 says that fingers are directions. The Śatapatha Brāhmaṇa (6.3.1.21 and 8.4.2.13) tells that the directions (Diśā) are ten. In modern scientific terminology direction will mean dimension. Thus we have evidence of universe being considered ten-dimensional in the Vedic cosmology. In the Vedic cosmology universe has a boundary which is obvious from the word "beyond" in this verse. Vāyu Purāṇa 4.82-84 tells us that the whole universe including the moon, sun, galaxies and planets was inside the egg and the egg was surrounded by ten qualities from outside. Vedic commentator Sāyaṇa also considers "dasāṅgula" to represent outside of the universe. This verse then tells us that outside of the universe is ten-dimensional. "Ten fingers" is not an isolated occurrence in the Vedas. Ten fingers extracting the juice of Soma is a recurring theme in the Ṛgveda (for example 9.46.6). It is also important to note that the same phenomenon has been described in various ways in the Ṛgveda. The aim is to make sure that important messages are not overlooked. So these ten fingers become ten women in Ṛgveda 9.56.3, where it is said that ten women call Soma to come to them. The Vedas are the source of many of our beliefs. When Hindus go to a foreign land, it is said that they have gone across the seven seas. Now the number of seas on our earth is not seven. This belief has its origin in "Sapta-sindhu" meaning seven rivers or seas of the Ṛgveda. The seven seas of the Ṛgveda have nothing to do with rivers or seas. Similarly Hindus still refer to forty nine winds. These forty nine winds have the origin in forty nine Marutas of the Ṛgveda, because Maruta means wind. However, Maruta has nothing to do with wind in the Ṛgveda. Hindus have the concept of ten directions. These ten directions are described as north, east, south, west, north-east, north-west, south-west, south-east, up and down. Obviously the counting of north-east, north-west, south-west and south-east as separate directions does not make sense at all. This is because the concept of ten directions has its origin in ten-dimensions of the Vedic physics, and when this knowledge was lost, Hindu intellectuals came up with the above explanation. Post-vedic Indian literature is full of such explanations of the Vedic knowledge, which do not make sense at all. There was little choice left to post-vedic Indian intellectuals, as the Vedic verses were becoming hard to comprehend. The Vedic science was being gradually forgotten, and in order to preserve the invaluable Vedic wisdom, some kind of explanation was necessary. The Brāhmaṇas have done the humanity a great service by preserving the Vedas against all odds. Today in the light of modern physics we can start the process of deciphering the Vedas.

"All this is Puruṣa, whatever has happened and whatever will happen. He is the lord of immortality, who increases by food." Ṛgveda 10.90.2

This verse is the origin of the Vedāntic philosophy. Chhāndogya Upaniṣad 3.14.1 says that all this is Brahma indeed. As everything in the universe is a manifestation of the Puruṣa, we are also part of the Supreme Being. Hindu scriptures tell us that when we realize the true nature of self, then there remains no difference between us and God. This realization is reflected in Bṛhadāraṇyaka Upaniṣad 1.4.10, which says that I am Brahma. The Puruṣa is not different from the universe. The universe is only a manifestation of him. This is why Hindus did not develop a dichotomy between good and evil as in other religions. There is no concept of eternal hell in Hinduism, because even hell cannot be separated from the God. In fact, there is no concept of hell or heaven after the end of the universe. The universe is only a manifestation of the Supreme Being and at the end of the present cycle of the universe called "Mahāpralaya" everything goes back into the Puruṣa. After the end of the universe, there is no heaven, there is no hell, and there are no souls.

Second part of the verse is very significant. It tells that Puruṣa is growing by food (Anna). Puruṣa also means a man. As a boy grows by eating food, the universe is growing by Anna. Obviously, this is no ordinary food (Anna). This food is the stuff that universe is made of. Thus "Anna" can be identified with the matter-energy of the universe. The expansion of universe is a key point of Vedic science, and is referred to again and again like in the present verse.

"Such is his glory. There is an even greater Puruṣa. All that is born, is his one fourth, his three fourth is immortal in heaven." Ṛgveda 10.90.3

The division of the universe in the earth and the heaven is the central thesis of the Vedic science. One fourth of universe is in the earth and three fourth of the universe is in heaven. This may look very unscientific, because the earth is negligibly small compared to the heaven. By no stretch of imagination earth can hold one fourth of the universe. However, I would remind my learned reader that knowledge of the Vedas is coded. Nothing in the Vedas means what it appears to mean. Once you understand the scientific meaning of the earth and the heaven, this verse will reveal a great cosmic secret. The meaning of the earth and the heaven will be discussed in detail in a later chapter. For those readers, who cannot hold their curiosity, there is a glossary at the end of the book, which lists the apparent meaning and scientific meaning of important technical terms used in the Vedas. I request the reader to frequently consult the glossary, whenever in doubt.

"Three-fourth of the Puruṣa is above. His one fourth is born again and again. Then he covered them all, those who eat, and those who don't." Ṛgveda 10.90.4

This verse reinforces the ideas of previous verse, so that there is no confusion about its meaning. One fourth of the Puruṣa is in the earth and is born repeatedly, while three fourth of the Puruṣa is in the heaven, where there is neither birth nor death. Earlier food (Anna) was identified with matter and energy of the universe, so eating refers to the transformation of matter into energy.

"Then Virāṭa was born. Virāṭa is greater Puruṣa. He began dividing after being born. Then Bhumi and Pura became." Ṛgveda 10.90.5

When universe starts to expand, it is given the name Virāṭa meaning extremely big. The expansion of universe is accompanied by its division in Earth and Heaven. Bhūmi refers to earth and Pura to the boundary of the universe. Pura means a fortified town and is also used in the sense of a fort surrounding the town. This concept is a very important one, as this will help unravel the meaning of the mightiest Vedic God, Indra, also called Purandara meaning one who breaks the fortified towns.

"When Gods started Yajña by oblation of the Puruṣa, spring was its butter, summer was fuel and winter was oblation." Ṛgveda 10.90.6

"That Puruṣa, who was born earlier, was sprinkled with sacrificial grass. Gods, Sādhyas and sages started the Yajña by the Puruṣa." Ṛgveda 10.90.7

These two verses talk about the Yajña, which is normally translated as sacrificial ceremony. The Puruṣa himself was sacrificed in this Yajña. The Yajña is a very important concept in Hinduism. The Yajña refers to the creation of matter, energy and space, none of which existed before the creation. My knowledgeable readers will object to this statement saying that matter and energy have always existed, and all the matter and energy of the entire universe was concentrated in a point before the

Big Bang. This is not the Vedic concept and I will argue in greater detail later in this book during the discussion of the Vedic cosmology that the universe did not start with a Big Bang. The Vedas are very clear about the universe emerging from a void (Śūnya), and this is the basis of the saying "Śūnya hī Parameśwara hai" meaning Void is God indeed.

As the universe had no matter, energy and space to begin with, the creation of these is obviously very important for the universe. As the Yajña is the creation of the stuff universe is made of, it is no wonder that the Vedic sages do not get tired of describing the importance of the Yajña. They declare that the Yajña is the navel of the universe, meaning the universe exists because of the Yajña. Śatapatha Brāhmaṇa 14.3.2.1 declares that the Yajña is the soul of all these beings.

"From that Yajña of entire offering coagulated butter (or butter mixed with curd) was obtained. Vāyavya, Āraṇya and Grāmya animals (Paśu) were made." Ṛgveda 10.90.8

As the Yajña proceeded, that is the creation of universe proceeded, the earlier homogeneous state became inhomogeneous. This inhomogeneity is represented by coagulated butter. The universe was no longer same everywhere. It separated into matter and energy. Matter particles were given the name animals, and divided in three categories: Grāmya meaning those living in villages, Āraṇya meaning wild animals, and Vāyavya meaning birds.

"From that Yajña of entire offering Ṛchas, Sāmas were born. From that meters (Chhandas) were born, from that Yaju was born." Ṛgveda 10.90.9

This verse is traditionally quoted to prove the origin of the Ṛgveda, the Sāmaveda, the Yajurveda, and the Atharvaveda from

God. The Atharvaveda is not explicitly mentioned and commonly Chhanda is identified with the Atharvaveda to prove the divine origin of the Atharvaveda. Of all four Vedas, the Ṛgveda is considered the most sacred and even other Vedas get their recognition of being divine by this verse in the Ṛgveda itself.

"From that horses were born, who have teeth on both sides. From that cows were born, from that goats and sheep were born." Ṛgveda 10.90.10

This verse sheds more light on Grāmya animals described earlier. Four Grāmya animals are listed here: horse, cow, goat and sheep. Vāyavya and Āraṇya animals are not listed

"The Puruṣa described here, how many ways has he been imagined? What (is) his mouth, what (are) both hands, what are called thighs and both legs?" Ṛgveda 10.90.11

"Brāhmaṇa was its mouth, Rājanya was made hands, its thighs (are) those that (are) Vaiśya, for both legs Śūdra is born." Ṛgveda 10.90.12

"From his mind the moon was born, from his eyes the sun was born. From his mouth Indra and fire (Agni) were born. From life-breath air (Vāyu) was born." Ṛgveda 10.90.13

"Atmosphere was from navel, from head came heaven. From both legs land, from ears directions (came), similarly worlds are imagined." Ṛgveda 10.90.14

These four verses are figurative, and describe the society and cosmos as various parts of the Supreme Being. The idea of God as a human being is described in a poetic way in these verses. These verses form the basis of the idea of God making man in his own image in Semitic religions.

"Seven were its enclosures (Paridhi). Three times seven were made firelogs (Samidha). In the Yajña, which gods were expanding, they sacrificed the Puruṣa-animal." Ṛgveda 10.90.15

This verse can be considered the key to understanding the Vedas. It contains the sacred numbers three and seven, both of which are encountered again and again in the Vedas. Three refers to the three Lokas, earth (Pṛthivī), atmosphere (Antarikṣa) and Heaven (Dyau). Each loka contains seven firelogs making the total twenty one.

What does the sacrifice of Puruṣa-animal mean? The sacrifice here means a change of form, a change from unmanifested form to a form of manifested universe. This change of form is described in a verse in the Atharvaveda:

"Earlier he had no legs, he gave rise to Svaḥ. He then became four-legged and consumable, later he ate all the food." Atharvaveda 10.8.21

When the Puruṣa is formless, he has no legs, when he takes form, he becomes legged. The consumption here represents the annihilation of particles into energy. At the end of the universe neither matter nor energy exists, which is represented as the Puruṣa having eaten all the food. As the Puruṣa ceased to be what the Puruṣa was before the creation, he was symbolically sacrificed. This has nothing to do with human sacrifice.

"Gods started the Yajña from Yajña, those were the first Dharmas. Those glorious ones attain heaven, where earlier celestial beings and gods are." Ṛgveda 10.90.16

Once the process of creation had started, it continued by itself. Vedic sages were worshippers of knowledge. They wanted their descendents to continue that tradition. Therefore they promised union with gods for those, who knew the process of creation.

3.2: Man in the image of God

As the Puruṣa hymn is the most important hymn in the Ṛgveda and the Ṛgveda was considered the most sacred knowledge by the inhabitants of the Indus Valley Civilization, it is natural to expect that the knowledge of the Puruṣa hymn will be reflected in their culture. Figure 3.1 shows the human figurine found at Mohenjo-daro in the Indus Valley. This has been called priest-king by Marshall, which is pure speculation. I will identify this with Puruṣa. First, this figure is indeed of a man, and Puruṣa means man. Second, the man is shown wearing a garment with three intersecting circles. These three intersecting circles represent the intertwined three lokas resulting from the two-fold division. The division of the universe in three spaces is discussed in detail in the sixth chapter. The Vedic ideas were spread all over the world during the dawn of human civilization. Later the origin of these ideas was forgotten, but the ideas were incorporated in the religions that came later. The depiction of God as man (Puruṣa) in the Ṛgveda is the basis of the belief in Semitic religions that man has been created in the image of God (Bible, Genesis 1.27).

3.3: Secret of the Unicorn

One of the most puzzling aspects of the Indus Valley Civilization is the depiction of a unicorn on the seals. There is no animal in the world that resembles the unicorn. Some historians have tried to explain it as a representation of a rhinoceros, but there is no similarity at all between a rhinoceros and the unicorn of the Indus Valley Civilization. Figure 3.2 shows the famous unicorn motif of Indus Valley Civilization. This is the motif of more than half of the seals found, so this is the central point of the belief of the Indus people. This also happens to be the representation of the fifteenth verse of the Puruṣa hymn.

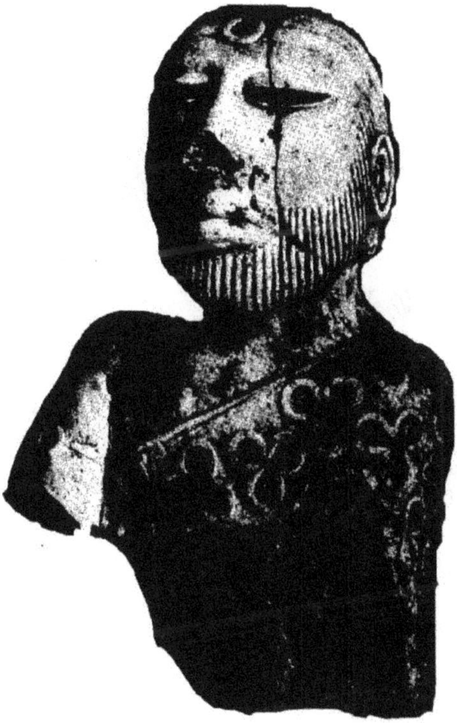

Figure 3.1: Puruṣa, a statue from Mohenjo-daro (DK 1909)

Figure 3.2: The sacrifice of the Puruṣa Animal, an Indus seal from Harappa (H-9)

The figure shows the sacrifice of the Puruṣa animal. In the verse Puruṣa is described as an animal, and so the seals represent the Puruṣa as an animal. But the Puruṣa is no ordinary animal. He is one lord of the whole universe. This oneness is represented by the one horn of the animal. A unicorn was also chosen to make the clear distinction that it does not represent an actual animal sacrifice, but is a symbolic one. The object in front of the unicorn is described in literature either as a mysterious object or a melange. It cannot be a melange as the mouth of unicorn is almost always facing away from the object. This object represents a Vadhyaśilā, a sacrificing stone on which the neck of sacrificed animal is put for slaughtering. The animal will obviously in such a situation look away from the stone. In some seals with this motif even few drops are visible, which would represent the blood coming out of sacrifice. The most important fact is that there is a direct correlation between the importance of the Puruṣa in the Vedas and the frequency of occurrence of seals with the unicorn motif.

The Puruṣa hymn is the most important hymn of the Vedas as attested by its occurrence in all four Vedas and description of its importance in post-vedic scriptures. That there is only one hymn dedicated to the Puruṣa in the Ṛgveda does not lessen the importance of the Puruṣa, because in the Ṛgveda all numbers are carefully selected. There is only one hymn dedicated to Puruṣa because there is only one Puruṣa. The unicorn motif is the most frequently depicted motif on the Indus seals, because it represents the sacrifice of the Puruṣa animal. This proves that the Indus Valley Civilization was Vedic Civilization.

3.4: Puruṣa sacrifice

As the Puruṣa hymn is the most important hymn of the Vedas, and knowledge of the Vedas was spread all over the world by ancient Indians, it is only to be expected that the myths related to the

Puruṣa sacrifice will be found all round the globe. In Egypt, the corpse of Osiris was torn in fourteen pieces and scattered all over. Various natural objects formed from these pieces. In Greek mythology, Dionysus Zagreus was chopped into pieces by the titans. In the Norse myths, giant Ymir is torn into pieces. Earth forms from his flesh, sea and waters from his blood, mountains from his bones, rocks from his teeth, plants from his hair, sky from his head, and clouds from his brain. Among Chaldeans, Omorca is cut in two pieces and two halves of her body became heaven and earth.

Among the Tinnehs, native Indian tribes of Canada, a giant tears apart a handsome young man. From the fragments thrown into the rivers fishes were born and from the fragments thrown into air birds were born [1]. Among Iroquois of North America, limbs, bones and blood of giant Chokanipok form natural objects.

3.5: The concept of paradise

Paradise is formed from the word Pairy-Diz meaning enclosure in the Avestā, an Iranian scripture having close resemblance to the Vedas. Pairy-Diz in turn is the deformation of Paridhi and has same meaning. As in the Puruṣa hymn, Pairy-Diz is also seven in the Avestā. This has given rise to the concept of seven tiers in heaven. Koran talks of seven heavens in 2.29, 67.3-5 and 71.15-16.

3.6: The Prajāpati

In the age of the Brāhmaṇas the concept of the Puruṣa was replaced by that of Prajāpati. The Śatapatha Brāhmaṇa says:

"Āpaḥ were indeed Salila earlier. Desire arose in it. They labored. From that heat arose. From heat golden egg was born. Golden egg was swimming in that for a year. After that year the Puruṣa was born. He is Prajāpati." Śatapatha Brāhmaṇa 11.1.6.1

In this mantra the Puruṣa is equated with the Prajāpati. In post-vedic scriptures the Prajāpati is the creator of the universe. We also see an important difference. The Puruṣa is shown as being born after the creation of the golden egg, which is clearly against what we have seen earlier in the Ṛgveda. The Śatapatha Brāhmaṇa is invaluable in our quest to find the meaning of the Vedas, but at the same time we have to be very careful in our attempt, because there is a clear sign of the loss of the Vedic science. The Brāhmaṇas are very clear about it themselves. After the Mahābhārata war, the Vedas started to become incomprehensible due to the loss of the Vedic knowledge base. The sages feared that soon the Vedas will become completely incomprehensible, and therefore they started to write the Brāhmaṇas, the commentaries on the Vedas. As such the Brāhmaṇas represent a significant deviation from the Vedas, and several centuries must have passed between the Mahābhārata war and the writing of the Brāhmaṇas.

In the Śatapatha Brāhmaṇa, the Prajāpati wants to cohabit with his daughter. She feels outraged and becomes a cow. The Prajāpati becomes a bull and cohabits with her. She keeps changing in to various animals, and the Prajāpati also keeps changing in to corresponding male animals. Thus various animals are born due to their cohabitation. There is a parallel Greek legend to this, in which Zeus takes the form of various animals. Persephone takes the form of a serpent and Zeus becomes a male dragon to cohabit with her. Similarly, Zeus took various animal forms of swan, eagle and dove in his amorous adventures. To woo the daughter of Cletor he became an ant. As these adventures are not found in the Vedas, it stands to reason that Greeks did not borrow these ideas from the Vedas, but from the Brāhmaṇas. This is only logical, because the Indus Valley Civilization is the Vedic civilization and predates Greek civilization by two millennia. The Greek civilization came into existence after the writing of the major Brāhmaṇas.

The Puruṣa hymn is the most important hymn of the Vedas, and the key to understanding the Vedic cosmology and the Indus Valley Civilization, therefore we will keep returning to the Puruṣa hymn throughout this book to unlock the secrets of the universe.

"Ptolemy created a universe that lasted a thousand years. Copernicus created a universe that lasted four hundred years. Einstein has created a universe, and I can't tell you how long it will last."

- George Bernard Shaw

4. THE EXPANDING EGG

Sanskrit is a beautiful language. Each word in Sanskrit tells its meaning itself. Each word has been thought carefully. Sanskrit is not a product of evolution from an earlier language. It has been designed to be what it is. When Vedic sages coded the knowledge of particle physics and cosmology, they were well aware of the possibility that one day the code may be lost due to the decline of their civilization. Therefore they chose the words very carefully to provide vital clues about the code. In this book we will dissect each word, go to its roots, and discover the lost Vedic science.

4.1: The expanding universe

The word for universe in Sanskrit is "Brahmāṇḍa", which is made by joining the words "Brahma" and "Aṇḍa". Brahma is derived from the root "Bṛha" meaning to expand and "Aṇḍa", which means egg. Thus "Brahmāṇḍa" means an expanding egg. The concept of the universe as an egg is found in nearly all ancient civilizations, the source of which is obviously the Ṛgveda. The concept of Martaṇḍa discussed later in this chapter is related to the egg-shaped universe. The universe is described as an egg in most post-vedic scriptures.

"Āpaḥ were indeed Salila earlier. Desire arose in it. They labored. From that heat arose. From the heat the golden egg was born. The golden egg was swimming in that for a year." Śatapatha Brāhmaṇa 11.1.6.1

"Whole universe including the moon, sun, galaxies and planets was inside the egg. The egg was surrounded by ten qualities from outside." Vāyu Purāṇa 4.82-84

"At the end of thousand years the Egg was divided in two by Vāyu" Vāyu Purāṇa 24.74

"From that golden egg the earth and heaven were made." Manusmṛti 1.13

In Matsya Purāṇa 2.25-30 following story is told about the creation. After Mahāpralaya, the dissolution of the universe, there was darkness everywhere. Everything was like in a state of sleep. There was nothing, either moving or unmoving. Then Swayaṃbhū, self-being, manifested, which is the form beyond senses. He created water first and established the seed of creation into it. That seed turned into a golden egg. Then Swayaṃbhū entered the egg, and he is called Viṣṇu because of entering. The concept of the universe as an egg is based on sound scientific reasoning. We will discuss the scientific basis of this shape later in this book during the discussion on the Vedic cosmology.

4.2: The birth of gods

What happened during the initial moments of creation? The Big Bang cosmology gives a very dramatic account of the first few moments. The universe was extremely hot and it went through a very rapid expansion stage initially called inflation. The Vedic viewpoint differs from this view. The initial moments of creation are described in the following hymn from the Ṛgveda:

Ṛgveda 10.72

Sage: Laukya Bṛhaspati or Bṛhaspatiraṅgirasa or Dākṣāyaṇī Aditi; Deity: Gods; Meter: Anuṣṭupa

1. We speak about the birth of Gods clearly. Who says the praises, will see them in later ages.
2. Brahmaṇaspati created these (everything in the universe) like an artisan. In the earlier age of gods manifest was born from unmanifest.
3. In the first age of gods, manifest was born from unmanifest. Then quarters of the heaven (Āśā) were born, after that one whose legs are extended.
4. From the one whose legs are extended, was born Bhū, and from Bhū were born quarters of the heaven (Āśā). From Aditi Dakṣa was born, and from Dakṣa Aditi was born.
5. Dakṣa, your daughter Aditi gave birth. Gracious, immortal bonded gods were born from her.
6. When gods were sitting in this Salila firmly established, from their dance penetrating dust came up.
7. When gods pervaded whole universe, then in the ocean sun was brought near.
8. Those eight sons born to Aditi, with seven she went to gods, and left Mārtaṇḍa away.
9. With seven sons Aditi went to an earlier age. For the birth and death of people, (she) accepted Mārtaṇḍa again.

4.3: The dead egg

The last two verses tell us about Mārtaṇḍa, and here lies the seed of a gigantic misconception that man was created in the beginning of the universe. Mārtaṇḍa means dead egg. Egg is the universe itself, so dead egg means a universe that had no life. The formation of universe was not a spontaneous process. The universe had to expand in order to exist, but the forces of expansion and contraction were in a delicate balance in the beginning. The universe did not keep on expanding continuously is the Vedic viewpoint. After an initial expansion, the universe started to contract. This is the meaning of Aditi going to earlier age. In the Śatapatha Brāhmaṇa there is an interesting story about Mārtaṇḍa.

"Aditi had eight sons. Only seven out of them were called Ādityas. Eighth Mārtaṇḍa did not have differentiated organs. Ādityas saw that he did not match with them, so they divided his organs. Then he turned into a man. He was named Vivasvāna and all people were born from him." Śatapatha Brāhmaṇa 3.1.3.3

Taittirīya Saṃhitā 6.5.6.1 says that Aditi gave birth to an immature egg. In Mahābhārata, Harivaṃśa Parva 9.5, Kaśyapa says to Aditi due to ignorance that her son is not dead, but he is inside the egg. Therefore he is called Mārtaṇḍa. The gist of all these stories is that the fundamental forces of nature were not fine tuned for the creation of the universe. After an initial expansion the universe started to collapse. Then the strengths of the fundamental forces were adjusted, and the universe began to expand again. Once the universe became steady, it was named Vivasvāna, where one could live. Śatapatha Brāhmaṇa 3.1.3.3 is the source of the myths that man was created in the beginning by God. It is important to note that Vivasvāna is the universe and he could not possibly give birth to human beings. In Ṛgveda 10.17.1 Yama has been called son of Vivasvāna, and in Ṛgveda 10.14.1 Yama has been called Vaivasvata meaning son of Vivasvāna. The sage of hymns 8.27-31 in the Ṛgveda is Vaivasvata Manu. Vaivasvata means son of Vivasvāna. In Indian scriptures Vivasvāna is father of Manu, first king, and in Iranian scripture Vīvaṅgahvanta (i.e.

Vivasvāna) is father of Yima (i.e. Yama), also the first king. Once the creation of human beings was accepted soon after the creation of universe in post-vedic literature, the Vedas were assumed to be delivered to human beings in the beginning. Though the knowledge contained in the Vedas is eternal, the Vedas were discovered by the sages of Indus-Saraswatī civilization. The universe is billions of years old, and the history of human civilization is only 10,000 years old. Before 10,000 years ago human mind was not developed enough to comprehend the knowledge contained in the Vedas. Human history, and obviously history of India as well, is only 10,000 years old, and the concept of Indian history being millions of years old as described in Purāṇas is wrong resulting from the confusion of the Vedic cosmology with human history. There is indeed human history in Purāṇas, but that starts only when Purāṇas stop describing the Vedic science as human history. This fact was indeed obvious to the authors of the Purāṇas. The Vedic concepts are very abstruse, and such abstruse concepts cannot keep ordinary people interested in Dharma, therefore the Purāṇas deliberately gave beautiful representations to these concepts. To ordinary Hindus they are spellbinding stories, but behind these stories is hardcore science, which educated Hindu is supposed to know. Unfortunately, long time back all Hindus forgot the science behind it, and then Hindus could no longer defend their Dharma from the onslaught of Christianity and Islam. The source of several ideas found in Christianity and Islam are Hindu scriptures, which have been borrowed without having the slightest idea about the real scientific meaning. In ancient and medieval world Hindus (including Buddhists) had spread their ideas far and wide. Consider the following expression from the Taittirīya Brāhmaṇa.

"After creating the universe and people, Prajāpati went to sleep."
Taittirīya Brāhmaṇa 1.2.6.1

Similar expression is also found in Bible (Genesis 2.2), which says that God rested on the seventh day after finishing all the work.

4.4: The Lord of expansion

Verse 10.72.2 tells that Brahmaṇaspati created the universe like an artisan. Brahmaṇaspati means the Lord of expansion. Thus Brahmaṇaspati can be identified with the expansion of the universe, and this mantra tells that universe was created due to the expansion. Another God in the Ṛgveda, who is used interchangeably with Brahmaṇaspati is Bṛhaspati, and the meaning of Bṛhaspati is also the same. Bṛhaspati in post-Vedic scriptures becomes the priest of the gods. Word Bṛhaspati has been used 128 times in the Ṛgveda and the word Brahmaṇaspati 49 times. Eleven complete hymns are dedicated to Bṛhaspati (1.40, 1.190, 2.23, 2.24, 2.25, 2.26, 4.50, 6.73, 10.38, 10.67 and 10.182) and in two other hymns (4.49 and 7.97) he has been praised along with Indra. Ṛgveda 2.24 describes the glorious deeds of Brahmaṇaspati.

Ṛgveda 2.24

Sage: Gṛtsamada Bhārgava Śaunaka; Deity: Brahmaṇaspati, 1, 10 – Bṛhaspati, 12 – Indra and Brahmaṇaspati;

Meter: Jagatī, 12, 16 – Triṣṭupa

1. Bṛhaspati, who rules the world, may he obtain our praises. We praise you by new great speeches, and your friend among us who praises you, may he refine our thoughts.
2. Brahmaṇaspati, who bent the bendable by his strength, who tore apart Śambaras in fury, who shook the unshakable, entered the Vasumanta mountain.
3. That is the work of the best god among the gods that firm became pliant, hard became soft. He brought cows out, killed Bala by Brahma, hid the darkness and lighted the heaven.

4. The well with the mouth of stone and stream of honey which Brahmaṇaspati broke by his strength, was drunk by sun's rays. He watered the streams a lot at once.
5. He opened the door of waters that have existed and that will form later, by months and years. The deeds that Brahmaṇaspati performed, one and the other use the waters effortlessly.
6. Searching on every side they discovered the remotest wealth hidden by Paṇis. Those wise ones after seeing the untruth, to enter it, went back to the place they had come from.
7. Truthful wise ones saw the untruth and stood on the great path again. They left Agni produced by their arms in the mountain, who was not there before.
8. Brahmaṇaspati uses bow with truth as string, wherever he wants, he pervades. Strings drawn to his ear he throws the successful arrows to see the men.
9. He organizes well, he leads well, he is well praised, he the priest Brahmaṇaspati fights well. When all-seeing holds strength and wealth, then sun heats up without effort.
10. All these first to be known riches, which both kinds of people enjoy, belong to rain-producing Brahmaṇaspati, who provides vast capabilities.
11. All pervading Brahmaṇaspati shows his greatness even in smaller fights. The god expands far bigger than other gods, and envelops them from all side.
12. Wealthy Indra and Brahmaṇaspati, laws of both of you always hold, even waters cannot violate your laws. Come straight towards our oblation and food like two horses connected to the chariot.
13. Fast moving horses hear, civilized wise people hold the wealth. May the strong, who is hostile to enemies, pay back

our debt. He, Brahmaṇaspati, is vigorous in hostile encounters.

14. Fury of Brahmaṇaspati, performer of great deeds, became true as he wished. He brought the cows out, divided them by great procedure for heaven, and they started moving separately by his power.
15. Brahmaṇaspati, let us be the master of all well regulated food and wealth, our braves procreate braves. O lord of all, may you hear our hymns.
16. Controller Brahmaṇaspati, may you know this hymn. Nourish our children. Whom gods protect, he is very fortunate. We having brave children will speak the great knowledge.

Verse two tells that Brahmaṇaspati entered Vasumanta mountain. There is no mountain by this name. In the Ṛgveda surface of the universe is called the mountain. Expansion of the universe is not spontaneous, and the energy barrier is represented by a mountain. Vasumanta means containing wealth, and thus this mountain is considered to have wealth hidden in it. This wealth is the matter and energy of the universe, which will manifest once the surface of the universe is pushed further back. In verse five Brahmaṇaspati is said to have opened the gates of waters. This is not ordinary water. The scientific meaning of these terms will become clear as we go along. In verse five Brahmaṇaspati is said to fight well. This fight is between the forces of expansion and contraction, and not between Aryans and Dravidians. In verse fourteen Brahmaṇaspati is said to free cows. Cows are often described in the Ṛgveda to be hidden in mountains, which are freed by Brahmaṇaspati.

"Cows hidden below were freed by two doors and cows above from one door." Ṛgveda 10.67.4

"When Bṛhaspati found the place where cows were hidden and making sound, cows came out of mountain like birds come out of egg." Ṛgveda 10.68.7

These cows are fundamental particles of nature, which are yet to manifest. In Ṛgveda 4.50.1 Bṛhaspati is called Triṣadhastha, i.e. staying in three places. These three places are earth, atmosphere and heaven. In Ṛgveda 4.50.4 Bṛhaspati is called first-born and having seven mouths. These seven mouths are seven dimensions of earth, atmosphere and heaven. We will take up the discussion of these dimensions later.

4.5: Puruṣa and Aditi

Most of the verses in the Vedas are mysterious. This is so because we don't know the actual scientific meaning of these verses. My aim in furnishing complete hymns is to give my learned readers as much information as possible, so that they can help in finding the lost Vedic science. One of these cosmic mysteries is of Aditi and Dakṣa giving birth to each other. This is impossible if they are considered human beings. Aditi is called the mother of the gods. In post-vedic scriptures Puruṣa and Aditi form a pair and become Viṣṇu-Lakṣmī or Śiva-Śakti. In Śiva Purāṇa, Dakṣa performs penance so that supreme mother Goddess Śakti could take human birth as his daughter Satī. This is only a representation of Aditi and Dakṣa giving birth to each other. Thus Purāṇas did an excellent job of bringing abstruse Vedic concepts in an interesting style to the ordinary Hindus, and succeeded in preserving the invaluable Vedic wisdom for thousands of years. The Vedas are books of science, which are fully capable of keeping people mesmerized by the knowledge they contain, but once the means to disseminate the scientific knowledge were lost, people started questioning the authority of the Vedas. In the changed circumstances, the Purāṇas came to the rescue of Hinduism. The wise sages transformed the

Vedic science in captivating stories to keep the ordinary Hindu interested in Dharma. Behind these stories there are all kinds of scientific information. Let's then go through a beautiful story of sage Agastya and his wife Lopāmudrā and see what is the science behind this story.

4.6: Agastya and Lopāmudra

Agastya is a very famous Vedic sage. He is credited with spreading of Aryan culture in south India. He is also supposed to be the author of first Tamil grammar. Agastya is derived from word Aga, which is formed by adding prefix "a" meaning negation to root "ga" meaning to go. Thus Agastya means one who does not move, i.e. remains fixed. The wife of sage Agastya is Lopāmudrā. Lopa means disappearance and mudrā means wealth, thus Lopāmudrā means disappeared wealth. Names in the Ṛgveda are not proper names, but they have a scientific meaning, which can be understood from its etymological meaning. The Ṛgveda is not about historical persons, but it tells the story of the evolution of the universe by personifying scientific phenomena. In Vedic cosmology the universe has a center, and the matter and energy is continuously being created at the surface of the universe as universe expands. Looking backward in time the universe had no matter and energy and space at time zero. There is a beautiful dialogue between Agastya and Lopāmudrā in first book of the Ṛgveda, which explains the story of creation.

Ṛgveda 1.179

Sage: 1, 2 – Lopāmudrā, 3, 4 – Maitrāvaruṇi Agastya, 5, 6 – disciple; Deity: Rati; Meter: Triṣṭupa, 5 – Bṛhatī

1. Lopāmudrā: I have been practicing self-restraint for several winters, getting old by the passage of days, nights and dawns.

Old age takes away the beauty of body. Vigorous should go near his wife (before that happens).

2. Lopāmudrā: Those truth-speaking people of past, who spoke truth with gods, could not find the end of restraint. Wife met the mighty husband.
3. Agastya: Our labor has not gone waste, because gods protect us. We have defeated all our enemies. Let's win the match of hundred tricks here. Let's meet like couple and produce children.
4. Agastya: Like a restrained river, desire has come to me from here, there and somewhere. Lopāmudrā is mating with strong husband. Fickle-minded is enjoying the composed taking long breaths.
5. Disciple: I pray to Soma, who is near and in my heart. If we have sinned, then may he forgive us, because mortals have many desires.
6. Disciple: Agastya excavated with spade desirous of children, descendents and strength. Fierce sage nourished the people of both color, and obtained true blessings among gods.

This dialogue is the representation of the early universe devoid of matter, energy and space. Lopāmudrā represents the state of vanished matter and energy and Agastya represents the fixed center of the universe. First verse tells that the expansion of the universe was not very rapid as in the inflationary Big Bang model. Instead there was a long incubation period before the expansion could become steady. It also says that the universe was cold in the beginning as opposed to infinitely hot universe of the Big Bang model. Third verse tells us that the battle between the forces of expansion and contraction has finally been decided in the favor of expansion, and the process of production of matter and energy is about to begin. Last two verses are told by a disciple of Agastya, who overheard the conversation between Agastya and Lopāmudrā. In verse five, Soma is considered near and inside. I will take up a detailed discussion of Soma later in the book. Forgiveness is asked from Soma, as Soma could have an adverse effect on creation. Sixth verse relates excavation with creation. This excavation is breaking up of mountains. The surface of the universe is represented as mountains, and expansion of universe is the excavation that results in the production of children, i.e. matter and energy. Most importantly, second half of the verse refers to production of children of two colors. What could be these two colors? Black and white, of course. These two colors represent matter and anti-matter. This disproves the myth of Aryan invasion, the myth of Aryans of fair complexion overpowering the dark-skinned Dravidians. In the Ṛgveda matter is represented as white and anti-matter is represented as black, the colors white and black were chosen to represent the opposite nature of matter and anti-matter. The Ṛgveda talks about the destruction of black-skinned people, but it is not about people, it is about annihilation of anti-matter. Our universe is matter-dominated and this could not have happened without the annihilation of anti-matter.

Now that you know the Vedic viewpoint that expansion of the universe was not spontaneous, you must be wondering what caused the expansion? What are the forces that create expansion and what are the forces that oppose it? The battle between the forces of expansion and contraction is an epic battle in the Ṛgveda, immortalized in the battle between Indra and Vṛtra, and the scene of this battle is the edge of the universe.

"For I can end as I began. From our home on earth we look out into the distances and strive to imagine the sort of world into which we are born. Today we have reached far out into space. Our immediate neighborhood we know intimately. But with increasing distance our knowledge fades, until at the last dim horizon, we search among ghostly errors of observations for landmarks that are scarcely more substantial. The search will continue. The urge is older than history. It is not satisfied and it will not be suppressed."

- Edwin Hubble

5. EDGE OF THE UNIVERSE

You have already seen that the universe has the shape of an egg and there is a boundary of the universe. Outside of the universe is ten-dimensional according to the Vedas. In contrast to the Vedic cosmology, the universe has no boundary in the Big Bang cosmology. The boundary of the universe is the scene of a fierce battle between the forces of expansion and contraction in the Vedic Cosmology. When this physics was forgotten, this battle became a battle between good and evil, between gods and demons, between God and Satan.

5.1: Indra and Vṛtra

The main force of expansion in the Vedic cosmology is Indra, and his chief adversary, the main force of contraction, is Vṛtra. Indra is often referred to as Purandara meaning one who breaks fortified towns (Pura). Pura is no ordinary town, but the entire universe, that is why the life principle of universe has been named Puruṣa. Thus Purandara means one who breaks the universe apart. Vṛtra means one who covers, and is derived from the root "Vṛ" to cover. If Indra is the one who breaks the universe apart, then his chief adversary Vṛtra must be the one who covers the whole universe. The Taittirīya Saṃhitā says that precisely.

"Vṛtra covered all three lokas." Taittirīya Saṃhitā 2.4.12.3

Three lokas constitute the universe, and therefore Vṛtra was covering the entire universe. If Vṛtra is located at the edge of the universe, then he can be said to be located very far away. One verse in Ṛgveda attests to this.

"Vṛtra was far above in Antarikṣa." Ṛgveda 2.30.3

The battle between Indra and Vṛtra has been described again and again in the Ṛgveda as this is the central point of Vedic cosmology. Let's then go through a Vedic hymn that describes this extraordinary battle in detail.

Ṛgveda 1.32

Sage: Hiraṇyastūpa Āṅgirasa; Deity: Indra; Meter: Triṣṭupa

1. Now I describe the glorious deeds of Indra, who holds Vajra. He killed the serpent and made waters flow. He broke the hearts of mountains.
2. He killed the serpent, which was taking refuge in mountain. Tvaṣṭā made the Vajra for him. Like the cows making sounds, flowing waters reached the sea.
3. Mighty Indra chose Soma, and drank from three containers. Generous Indra held Vajra in his hand, and killed first born among the serpents.

4. O Indra, when you killed first born among the serpents, you also made the deception of deceivers ineffective. Then you created dawn and sun in heaven, afterwards you could not find any enemy.
5. Indra severed and killed the great coverer Vṛtra by mighty devastating Vajra. Like a trunk of a tree cut down by axe, serpent was lying on earth.
6. Unlike a good warrior, arrogant engaged the mighty warrior, expeller of enemies, who can subdue several opponents. Enemy of Indra could not withstand the devastating blows of Indra, and broke into several pieces at once.
7. Without leg and without hand, Vṛtra fought Indra. Indra hit him by Vajra on his head. Like a weakling fighting a mighty warrior, Vṛtra was lying scattered at several places.
8. Like the river overflowing its banks, waters started to flow recklessly over lying Vṛtra. Whom Vṛtra was holding by his great extent, the serpent was trampled under their feet.
9. Mother of Vṛtra became weak. Indra attacked below her. Then mother was on top and son was below. Like a cow over her calf, Dānu was lying.
10. Body was lying among the water-streams, which never stop and never rest. Waters were flowing over the hidden Vṛtra. The enemy of Indra was lying in deep darkness.
11. Wife of Dāsa and protected by serpent, waters were held back like cows by Paṇi. The gate holding waters was closed. Indra killed Vṛtra and opened them.
12. When Vṛtra counterattacked, one god Indra became the hair of horse. Mighty Indra won the cows, won Soma, and freed seven rivers to flow.

13. Neither lightening, nor thunder was successful for him. Neither fog nor hail was successful. When Indra and serpent fought, generous Indra won for coming years.
14. O Indra, which follower of serpent did you see that fear entered the heart of the slayer of Vṛtra? You crossed nine and ninety streams like a terrified eagle.
15. Indra, who holds Vajra in his hand, is the king of moving and stationary, of peaceful and horned animals. He is the king of men. He is enveloping like the felly of wheel surrounds spokes.

It is clear from these verses that Vṛtra is same as the serpent. The serpent was holding the waters, which was freed when the serpent Vṛtra was slain. Vṛtra was not holding an ordinary amount of water. Verse 12 tells us that slaying of Vṛtra resulted in freeing seven rivers to flow. Freeing of seven rivers by Indra in this verse is not an isolated example, but is repeated several times in Ṛgveda. The Vedic idea of a serpent holding all the waters is found in different myths all over the world.

5.2: Frog who drank all the waters

The myth of a frog that drank all the waters is found among North American Indian tribe Algonkins, Australian Indians and Andaman Islanders [1]. Algonkins myth relates to the story of a man named Ioskeha. The earth was earlier arid and sterile. Ioskeha killed the gigantic frog that had swallowed all the waters. The waters were released and Ioskeha guided the waters in to smooth streams and lakes. According to an Australian myth, a huge frog was holding all the waters, and there was no water available anywhere on earth. Frog was made to laugh and waters ran out of its mouth. In the myth of Andaman Islanders, a toad drank up all the waters, and there was a drought. When the toad started to dance, the waters gushed out of its mouth. The source of all these myths is the legendary battle of Indra with Vṛtra. As the myth spread, the serpent turned into a frog, but the basic idea of a serpent holding all the waters remained the same.

5.3: Electric force

Having realized that the battle between Indra and Vṛtra is the battle between the forces of expansion and contraction, it is now time to pinpoint which forces are represented by Indra and Vṛtra. Modern science talks of three fundamental forces in nature: gravitation, strong nuclear and electroweak. The force of gravitation is the force between any two masses and is always attractive. It is the force that acts over long range and holds solar system and galaxies together. Indra cannot be the force of gravitation, as gravitation is an attractive force. Strong nuclear force is responsible for keeping atomic nucleus together, thus Indra cannot be this force either, because the force represented by Indra must be long range. Electroweak force consists of weak nuclear force and electromagnetic force. Weak nuclear force is a very short-range force acting at a distance of around 10^{-18} meter, and we are considering here a force that acts on a cosmic scale. Thus weak nuclear force is also ruled out. Electromagnetic force consists of electric force and magnetic force. Both of these forces can be either attractive or repulsive and can act over long distances. Indra will be identified here as electric force based on further evidence in the Vedic literature. In Ṛgveda 4.17.13 Indra has been called "Aśanimāna" meaning one who possesses thunderbolt. Furthermore, Kauśītaki Brāhmaṇa 6.9 says that Indra is Aśani (thunderbolt). The Śatapatha Brāhmaṇa says:

"Who is Indra and who is Prajāpati? Thunder is Indra and Yajña is Prajāpati." Śatapatha Brāhmaṇa 11.6.3.9

Thus it becomes clear that Indra is related to electrical phenomena and his identification with electric force is on solid grounds.

5.4: Surface tension

Our next agenda should be to identify Vṛtra. We know that Vṛtra covers the whole universe and is a force of contraction. This brings immediate realization that Vṛtra is none other than the surface tension of the universe. A drop of fluid tends to become spherical in order to minimize its surface area. There is energy associated with every surface, and every system tries to minimize its energy. This is why bubbles are spherical, because sphere is the configuration of the lowest surface area. If the universe is trying to expand, its surface area is going to increase, which will increase the total surface energy of the universe. The surface tension will act to minimize the surface area of the universe, in other words the surface tension will try to contract the universe. The electric repulsion force must be stronger than the surface tension force in order for the universe to expand. This is the grand cosmic battle of Indra and Vṛtra, and it is given so much prominence in the Ṛgveda for the reason that outcome of this battle determines whether there will be a universe or not. The Ṛgveda describes this grand battle in various ways, one of them is the killing of wild boar.

5.5: Slaying of Varāha

Varāha has the apparent meaning of wild boar. It is derived from root "Vṛ" and etymologically means one who covers. Thus etymological meanings of Varāha and Vṛtra are same, and it is not a coincidence that Ṛgveda describes the killing of Varāha as well as Vṛtra. The slaying of Varāha is attributed to Viṣṇu and Trita.

"Viṣṇu killed Varāha and stole cooked food" Ṛgveda 1.61.7

"Trita, strengthened by Indra, killed Varāha using iron fingernails." Ṛgveda 10.99.6

Varāha and Vṛtra both represent the surface of the universe. Trita is said to have fingernails of iron, which represents the magnetic properties of Trita. Some of the readers, who know about modern cosmological theories in detail, might be considering this discussion on surfaces absurd, as universe is not supposed to have any surface in the first place. The reality is scientists have already found the evidence of surface phenomena at work on cosmological scales, but have failed to identify it as such. Scientists have recently found bubbles and voids at cosmic scale, a hallmark of surface tension at work.

5.6: Bubbles and voids in space

One of the most important assumptions underlying Big Bang cosmology is that universe is uniform everywhere. This means that all parts of universe have same mass-energy density and structure. In such considerations, choosing the appropriate unit of mass-energy dispersion becomes important. We know that planets and stars are not uniformly distributed. Scientists chose a larger scale, and at first believed that galaxies are spread uniformly over space. When Hubble conducted a survey of 44,000 galaxies, he did not find them uniformly distributed, instead he found considerable clustering. His survey was followed by that of Fritz Zwicky in 1938 and again it was found that galaxies were clumped, and not uniformly distributed. This finding gave rise to the consideration that cluster of galaxies is an appropriate unit, and that clusters of galaxies are spread uniformly over space. Our galaxy, Milky Way, is part of a cluster of twenty five galaxies. French astronomer Gerard de Vaucouleurs conducted a survey on an even bigger scale in 1950, and found that even clusters of galaxies were not uniformly distributed. He grouped clusters of galaxies in superclusters spreading 200 million light years. Scientists soon came to believe that supercluster was the appropriate unit over which universe looked uniform. Probing even further scientists have recently found that superclusters are located over the surface of giant bubbles. Inside of the bubbles are large voids containing no galaxies, almost bereft of matter and energy. We have a reference to this large scale structure in the Śatapath Brāhmaṇa:

"When Āpaḥ were heated, foam (Phena) was created." Śatapatha Brāhmaṇ 6.1.3.2

Āpaḥ means water and its scientific meaning will be discussed in the chapter "Return of the Elements". There are ample references to prove that the Vedic sages considered Āpaḥ to pervade whole universe. Not knowing the real meaning of Āpaḥ, all religions and mythologies talk of a universe filled with water in the beginning. The verse quoted above clearly proves that Vedic sages considered surface phenomena to be at work, so that Āpaḥ were organized as foam. The finding of bubbles on the large scale structure of universe is a clear proof to me that surface tension has been at work during the evolution of the universe. As modern scientists have failed to take the surface tension in account, it is no wonder that the Big Bang cosmology cannot predict the evolution of the galaxies. The reason is clear. Whole framework of the Big Bang cosmology is wrong. The chapters on the Big Bang and the Vedic cosmology discuss this further.

5.7: Deeds of Indra

More than 250 hymns have been dedicated to Indra in the Ṛgveda. Another fifty plus hymns sing the praises of Indra in combination with other gods like Vāyu, Varuṇa, Agni, Viṣṇu, Soma and Bṛhaspati. Vedic sages do not get tired of describing the glorious deeds of Indra. More than one fourth of the Ṛgvedic verses are about Indra. The hymn traditionally considered the most favorite hymn of Indra is presented below. This hymn being the most important hymn about Indra is helpful in understanding Indus Valley Seals as well.

Ṛgveda 2.12

Sage: Gṛtsamada Bhārgava Śaunaka; Deity: Indra; Metre: Triṣṭupa

1. Who is first among the gods, who after being born adorned gods from his actions, from whose impulse earth and heaven tremble, who is famous for his strength, he, O people, is Indra.
2. Who made the trembling earth firm, who pacified the angry mountains, who measured the wide atmosphere, who supported the heaven, he, O people, is Indra.
3. Who killed the serpent and made seven rivers flow, who got the cows hidden by Bala out, who created Agni between two rocks, who kills enemies in wars, he, O people, is Indra.
4. Who has made the shaking world, who has put Dāsa varṇa in a hidden place below, who conquers like the hunter killing dogs, the lord who snatches nourishing material from enemies, he, O people, is Indra.
5. About whom people ask where is the awful, and say that he does not exist, he the lord destroys nourishing material of enemies, so have respect for him, because he, O people, is Indra.
6. Who instigates rich and poor, knowledgeable, needy and poet, who has beautiful cheeks, who protects those extracting Soma juice using stones, he, O people, is Indra.

7. Whose horses are, whose cows are, whose villages are, whose all chariots are, who created sun and Uṣā, who leads the waters, he, O people, is Indra.
8. Whom earth and heaven moving together call for help, whom high and lowly both enemies call, whom two warriors sitting on the same chariot call in several ways, he, O people, is Indra.
9. Without whose help people can't win, whom warriors call for protection, who became world's model, who moves the unmovable, he, O people, is Indra.
10. Who kills the sinners and ignorant by Vajra, who does not let the arrogant win, who kills the Dasyus, he, O people, is Indra.
11. Who found Śambara hiding in the mountains during fortieth winter, who killed the valiant serpent and sleeping Dānu, he, O people, is Indra.
12. Who is seven-rayed strong bull, who freed seven rivers for flowing, who holding Vajra in his hand killed Rohaṇa riding on heaven, he, O people, is Indra.
13. For whom earth and heaven bow, whose strength mountains fear, who drinks and protects Soma, who holds Vajra in his hand, he, O people, is Indra.
14. Who protects those extracting and cooking Soma juice, who protects those reciting hymns and those active in worship, who increases by hymns, whose Soma is, whose wealth is, he, O people, is Indra.

In verse three Indra is credited with getting the cows hidden by Bala out. Elsewhere in Ṛgveda Indra is said to have killed Bala and freed the cows hidden in mountains (Ṛgveda 1.11.5, 2.14.3, 8.14.8). Similarly, Indra frees cows well hidden in rocks (Ṛgveda 5.30.4, 6.43.3). According to Ṛgveda 6.39.2 Indra breaks apart mountains. This mountain is the surface of the universe. I have also earlier shown that Vṛtra is the surface of the universe. Maitrāyaṇī Saṃhitā 4.5.1 shows the equivalence of mountain and Vṛtra by saying "Girir vai Vṛtro", meaning mountain is indeed Vrtra. In Vedic cosmology the surface of the universe is mountain, and the seven rivers of Ṛgveda originate from this mountain, i.e. surface of the universe. The cows hidden in mountain are not ordinary cows. In Ṛgveda Indra is shown as having affection for cows, and this quality later on passes to Lord Viṣṇu during the age of the Purāṇas.

"Indra desires to obtain cow." Ṛgveda 8.17.15

"Indra always wins the battle for cows." Ṛgveda 4.17.10, 4.21.4

"Indra loves cows." Ṛgveda 1.84.11

The shelter for cows is called Gotra in Sanskrit. Gotra is same as the mountains which Indra breaks (Ṛgveda 1.51.3, 3.30.21, 3.43.7, 4.16.8, 10.103.7). This is why he is called Gotrabhid, breaker of Gotra, in Ṛgveda 2.23.3, 6.17.2, 10.103.5. It is due to his association with cows, that Indra is called bull in the Vedas.

5.8: Indra, the Bull

Asko Parpola in his book "Deciphering the Indus script" describes an amulet from Harappa (3305) showing a deity with bull's legs and a raised club [2]. Surprisingly he does not give any clue as to what this figure could represent. Proponents of the Aryan Invasion Theory use the Vedas, Brāhmaṇas, Upaniṣads and Purāṇas selectively to prove that the Indus Valley Civilization was Dravidian Civilization. For this reason, they find representation of Rudra and Varuṇa in the Indus seals, because Rudra and Varuṇa have already been declared as a borrowing from the Indus Valley Civilization. In fact, there is no such thing as borrowing from Indus Valley Civilization, because Indus Valley Civilization was the Vedic Civilization. This amulet 3305 from Harappa is proof of my thesis. The deity has bull's legs, and Indra is considered bull in the Vedas. In Ṛgveda 2.12.12 Indra is called a bull, and so in other Vedas.

"Bull is the form of Indra." Atharvaveda 9.4.7-8

The deity also has a raised club in one of his hands. Now, Vedas repeatedly describe Indra as holding Vajra is his hand. Thus, there is no room to doubt that this figure is the representation of Indra. And with this identification, we have buried the Aryan Invasion Theory and the thesis of Indus Valley Civilization being Dravidian. There is no way representation of Indra in Harappa can fit in these theories. Indra is supposed to have destroyed this civilization, how could these people be worshipping him? The mighty deeds of Indra were known all over the world and people worshipped Indra everywhere albeit under different names.

5.9: Mighty Hercules

Magi of Asia minor identified the Iranian god Verethraghna with Greek Heracles, who later became Roman Hercules. Verethraghna is only a deformation of Vṛtrāghna meaning slayer of Vṛtra. Iranians forgot Indra, but turned one of his adjectives in a heroic god.

5.10: Serpent as evil

You might be wondering why Vedic sages describe Vṛtra as a serpent. A serpent does something very important several times during its lifetime. It changes its skin. What about the universe? As universe expands, its surface is destroyed, but another surface is created instantly. In effect universe keeps changing its skin. Thus the battle between Indra and Vṛtra never stops. It carries on all the time. This is also one reason that this battle is described all through the Ṛgveda again and again and again. My opinion is that the Ṛgveda contains the information on evolution of the universe as it has happened, and divided the evolution in seven important phases, each phase being described by one of the seven sages. The slaying of Vṛtra has an interesting counterpart in mythology. Vṛtra never dies as universe always has a surface. In mythology also one encounters demons that rise from dead again and again. The depiction of Vṛtra as a serpent and an enemy of Indra made the serpent as a symbol of evil all over the ancient world, as Vedic ideas were spread far and wide.

In Bible, Satan is depicted as a serpent, who induces Eve to eat the forbidden apple (Genesis 3.1-15). The depiction of serpent as a force of evil is based on the Vedic description of Vṛtra as a serpent. In Greek mythology, the fight between Indra and Vṛtra becomes the fight between Apollo and Pytho. Pytho, the great serpent, had swallowed all the waters just like Vṛtra, before he was slain. After the slaying Apollo also fled in terror just like Indra did (Ṛgveda 1.32.14). Apollo was also considered Sun-god just like Indra during the period of the Brāhmaṇas. We should note here that Indra is not a Sun-god in the Ṛgveda. In another version, the epic war becomes the fight between Perseus and Medusa, who carries several snakes on her head.

Back home in India, serpent did not become a force of evil. After all, here it was well known that this battle was not about good and evil. Indra and Vṛtra both have important places in the evolution of the cosmos. In later mythology serpent on one hand became the garland of Lord Śiva, and on the other hand became the companion of Lord Viṣṇu. The serpent became Śeṣanāga, a serpent with several heads. Lord Viṣṇu rests on the bed of his coils and Śeṣanāga also provides shade to Lord Viṣṇu by spreading his heads above. Thus Śeṣanāga covers Lord Viṣṇu the same way Vṛtra covers the universe. We should remember that in Hinduism universe is not different from God. In Vedic science, the universe has a tripartite division into earth, atmosphere and heaven and in this division lies the ultimate secret of the universe.

"Observations are to be regarded as discrete, discontinuous events. Between these are gaps which we cannot fill in."
- Erwin Schrödinger

6. PARALLEL SPACES

The tripartite division of universe in Pṛthivī (earth), Antarikṣa (atmosphere) and Dyau (heaven) is very well established in the Vedic literature. Each of them is called a "Loka" and thus universe is "Triloka", consisting of three lokas. Therefore God is called "Trilokīnātha" meaning lord of three lokas. Pṛthivī means the broad and extended one, Antarikṣa means what exists in between, and Dyau means bright. Like other technical words in Vedas, these three words have exact scientific meaning different from their apparent meaning. These three lokas were formed by the division of the egg-shaped universe.

"At the end of thousand years Egg was divided in two by Vāyu" Vāyu Purāṇa 24.74

The universe was divided in two. This division is like a change of phase of chemical substances. Consider a fluid that transforms into a solid and liquid phase due to change in temperature. Whenever two phases are formed, there is always an interface between these phases. Antarikṣa is the interface between Pṛthivi and Dyau. Taittirīya Upaniṣad 1.3.1 says that Antarikṣa is the junction of Pṛthivī and Dyau. The Śatapatha Brāhmaṇa says:

"These lokas were together in the beginning. Earth and heaven then separated and the space between them became Antarikṣa." Śatapatha Brāhmaṇa 7.1.2.23

Three lokas were formed not because the universe was divided in three, but because it was divided in two. Should the interface be considered a separate phase? Scientists are divided on this issue. Gibbs does not consider interface to be a separate phase and instead draws an imaginary plane through the interface dividing the phases in two. Guggenheim on the other hand considers interface to be a separate phase, and assigns all the properties to an interface that a phase can have [1].

The most important concept of the Vedas is the division of universe. Without a proper understanding of this division the Vedas will seem meaningless. How was the egg divided? Was it divided in an upper half and lower half? To answer this question let's consider the first verse of Puruṣa hymn again.

6.1: Three spaces

"Puruṣa has thousand heads, thousand eyes and thousand legs. He is covering Bhūmi from all around, and is beyond also in ten-finger form." Ṛgveda 10.90.1

You have already seen that Bhūmi here means entire universe. Bhūmi and Pṛthivī have similar meaning and have been used interchangeably in the Vedas. In Ṛgveda 10.81.3 the word "Dyāvābhūmi" has been used, while in most places "Dyāvāpṛthivī" is used. Sāyaṇa in his commentary on Atharvaveda 6.18.2 says that Bhūmi is Pṛthivī. Sāyaṇa in his commentary (Ṛgveda Bhāṣya) on Ṛgveda 10.90.1 and Mahīdhara in his commentary (Yajurveda Bhāṣya) on Yajurveda 39.1 say that "Bhūmim

Brahmāṇḍagolakarūpam" meaning Bhūmi is the round universe. Thus I am on very solid grounds to consider Pṛthivī as the universe. If Pṛthivī is the universe, then what are Antarikṣa and Dyau? After all, the universe consists of Pṛthivī, Antarikṣa and Dyau. I hope my readers can guess where my arguments are headed. The egg was not divided in upper half and lower half, but in an intermingled web. It is a web that pervades the whole universe. This web is what is considered Māyājāla meaning a measured web. Māyā is a powerful term in Hinduism, which has now come to mean an illusion that the universe is. However, Māyā is formed from root "mā" to measure, and could not have meant illusion originally. The universe is made on scientific principles, and that's why it is well measured. Universe consists of three intertwined webs, Pṛthivī, Antarikṣa and Dyau. Pṛthivī can be given a scientific name "observer space". Pṛthivī is our space, the space in which we live and die, whatever we can see and observe. Earth, sun, stars, galaxies all are part of Pṛthivī. From one end of the universe to the other end is the expanse of Pṛthivī, and that is what the name Pṛthivī means: the broad and extended one. Dyau will be termed "Light space" because light propagates in this space as you will find in more detail later, and Antarikṣa will be termed "Intermediate space" as this space exists in between observer space and light space. Pṛthivī, Antarikṣa and Dyau exist at every point in space. If we could make a powerful microscope that could make observations at the most subtle level, then we will see space divided in three strands belonging to observer space, intermediate space and light space. A verse from Yajurveda clearly states that division of universe was done on a very subtle level, and not on a gross level.

"I place earth and heaven inside you. I place wide atmosphere inside you." Yajurveda 7.5

Vedic sages had the capability of looking at such a subtle level, which is beyond the reaches of modern science. The concept of Kośas is related to observations at different scales. Taittirīya Upaniṣad 2.2-3 describes the various levels of observation. The grossest level of observation is called Annamaya Kośa, which corresponds to macroscopic observation. Praṇamaya Kośa refers to observations at a level more subtle than Annamaya Kośa. This may be referring to microscopic observation. Next three levels of observation in order of subtlety are Manomaya Kośa, Vijñānamaya Kośa and Ānandamaya Kośa.

At present, modern science is not capable of observing at such subtle scales. Our observations are limited to observer space, in extreme cases our observations can reach the intermediate space, but our observations never reach the light space, which is hidden very deep. These three spaces are the three legendary steps of Viṣṇu in the Ṛgveda.

6.2 The steps of Viṣṇu

Viṣṇu, Brahmā and Maheśa form a trinity in Hinduism. Form of Viṣṇu in the Purāṇas is slightly different from that in Vedas. Viṣṇu is a friend of Indra in the Ṛgveda, who helps Indra in the slaying of Vṛtra. Though hymns dedicated to Viṣṇu are few in the Ṛgveda, this does not mean that Viṣṇu has less significance in the eyes of the Vedic sages. In Ṛgveda number of hymns and mantras are carefully chosen. Three complete hymns have been dedicated to Viṣṇu in Ṛgveda (1.154, 1.156, 7.100), which correspond to the three spaces of the universe. There are few mantras separately for Viṣṇu (1.22.17-22, 1.155.4-6, 7.99.1-3, 7.99.7). He is also invoked with other gods in some hymns and mantras (Ṛgveda 1.22.16, 1.155.1-3, 5.3.3, 6.69, 7.99.4-6). Viṣṇu is derived from root "Viṣ" meaning to enter or pervade, and he is called so because he pervades the whole universe. Brahmāṇḍa Purāṇa 1.4.25 says that he is called Viṣṇu because he has entered in everything. Three steps of Viṣṇu are referred to several times in the Vedas (Ṛgveda 1.22.17, 1.154.3, 1.155.4, Sāmaveda 2.10.20, Atharvaveda 7.26.5). What are his three steps? Vājasaneyī Saṃhitā (2.25, 5.14) and Śatapatha Brāhmaṇa (1.1.2.13, 1.9.3.9, 3.6.3.3) identify three steps as heaven, atmosphere and earth. Taittirīya Saṃhitā 2.4.12 says that Viṣṇu established his one third in earth, one third in atmosphere and one third in heaven. Obviously, earth, atmosphere and heaven were considered to be of comparable extent. The most important aspect of Viṣṇu's three steps is that whole universe is covered by these steps.

Śatapatha Brāhmaṇa 1.2.5.1-7 tells a story about three steps of Viṣṇu. Devas (gods) and Asuras (demons) were sons of Prajāpati, and were always fighting each other. Once Devas became weak and Asuras captured the earth. Asuras started to divide earth among them. Then Devas brought Viṣṇu forward and asked for his share. Asuras saw that Viṣṇu is a dwarf, so they agreed to give Viṣṇu as much land as he could occupy by his body. Devas thought that Viṣṇu is Yajña, so if Asuras gave land equal to him, then they have given whole earth. They enclosed Viṣṇu with meters and started to expand the Yajña. Devas thus obtained whole earth for themselves. This story further develops in Purāṇas, Mahābhārata and Rāmāyaṇa. Asura Bali was performing a Yajña, which will give him unlimited powers. Devas went to Viṣṇu and ask for help. Viṣṇu took birth as son of Kaśyapa and Aditi. He did not grow much and remained a dwarf. In this form he went to Bali and asked for land. Bali agreed to give him as much land as he could occupy in three steps. Viṣṇu measured the whole universe in his three steps and Devas became master of the universe again. In some Purāṇas, Viṣṇu covered the whole universe in only two steps, and there was nothing left for third step.

Viṣṇu can be identified with universe itself. This dwarf incarnation refers to the early universe, when universe was very small. Viṣṇu's first step is the observer space, his second step is the intermediate space, and his third and remotest step is the light space. We get further proof of this in Vedas. In his three steps rests the whole universe (Ṛgveda 1.154.2, Vājasaneyī Saṃhitā 23.49). The most notable aspect of Viṣṇu's three steps is that third step is considered very remote and beyond the reach of anyone. His two steps can be known by humans, but third step is beyond the sight of humans and flight of birds (Ṛgveda 1.155.5). Wise people know earth and atmosphere, but Viṣṇu knows the remotest (Ṛgveda 7.99.1). In Ṛgveda 1.155.3 heaven is explicitly referred as Viṣṇu's third abode. Light space (Dyau) cannot be observed by humans. If Dyau meant heaven in Vedas, this won't make any sense, as constituents of heaven like sun and stars are easily seen by human eyes. Among the brave acts of Viṣṇu in the Ṛgveda is the slaying of wild boar.

"Viṣṇu killed Varāha and stole cooked food" Ṛgveda 1.61.7

The slaying of wild boar (Varāha) has been discussed in the last chapter. Varāha represents the surface of the universe. As Viṣṇu (the universe) expands, surface of the universe is broken, and thus Varāha is killed. Ironically in the Purāṇas, Viṣṇu takes incarnation as a Varāha. There is a different scientific explanation for the incarnations of Viṣṇu, which is discussed in a later chapter. In the Ṛgveda, Indra and Viṣṇu are shown as close friends. Viṣṇu and Indra expand the spaces in Ṛgveda 6.69.5. In the Brāhmaṇas, Viṣṇu comes to mean the sun as the youngest son of Aditi, but there is no reason to suspect such identification in the Vedas. Viṣṇu is clearly depicted as being different from Sūrya (sun) in Ṛgveda 7.99.4.

6.3: The hidden spaces

There are several verses in Vedas that support the interpretation of Pṛthivī, Antarikṣa and Dyau as the observer space, intermediate space and light space respectively. Pṛthivī and Dyau are described as following:

"One of them is hidden and other is observable. There ways are same still divided differently." Ṛgveda 3.55.15

All three spaces are described beautifully in the following verse:

"Continuously moving, very wide three are positioned one on top of another. Two of them are hidden and only one is seen." Ṛgveda 3.56.2

Intermediate space and light space are considered hidden, which is completely true. We can spend our lifetimes without ever realizing that these two spaces even exist. Out of these two, the light space is considered hidden deeper than intermediate space. All through the Ṛgveda we come across references to the hidden space. A verse from the Ṛgveda proclaims:

"Agni, I know your three places and three forms. I know your place that is protected in various ways. I know your name that is in a very secret place, I know the place from which you have been born." Ṛgveda 10.45.2

Here three places of Agni are the observer, intermediate and light spaces, and his three forms are Agni (fire), Vāyu (air) and Sūrya (sun) respectively. The very secret place is the light space, and Agni's name in that place is Sūrya. The place from which Agni is born is the golden womb.

In Ṛgveda 1.159.4 earth and heaven are described by following epithets: "Jāmī sayonī mithunā samokasā". Jāmī means siblings, sayonī means born from the same womb, mithunā means couple, and samokasā means having same abode. This explicitly refers to being born together, lying one top of other like a couple and being spread all through the universe. The concept of Dyau as the hidden space is the most important concept of the Vedic science without understanding which Vedas will seem meaningless. The Ṛgveda itself states this in no uncertain terms.

"Vedic mantras are in the never-decaying remotest sky, where all the gods reside. One who does not know that, what will he do with Vedic mantras? One who knows that, they (gods) stay with him." Ṛgveda 1.164.39

The remotest sky is the light space, which is the abode of energy. Now that we have a precise understanding of what earth and heaven represent, this is the right time to appreciate a beautiful hymn dedicated to them.

Ṛgveda 1.185

Sage: Agastya Maitrāvaruṇi; Deity: Dyāvāpṛthivī; Metre: Triṣṭupa

1. Which was born first and which later? How were they born? Who knows O wise people? They hold the universe by their strength and always keep rotating like a wheel.

2. Two unmoving without legs hold many moving, with legs, in their womb. May heaven and earth protect us from sin like parents protect the son near them always.

3. I ask for the sinless, never diminishing, bright, non-violent donation of Aditi. May heaven and earth produce that wealth for the worshipper. May heaven and earth protect us from sin.

4. Heaven and earth, parent of gods, protect people without becoming angry. May we with day and night of gods retain the favor of both. May heaven and earth protect us from sin.

5. Two young ladies always moving together, having the ends together, sisters, staying near father, smell the center of universe. May heaven and earth protect us from sin.

6. I call by truth the wide, great, provider of space, progenitors of gods for protection. The beautiful ones hold immortality. May heaven and earth protect us from sin.

7. I bow and praise wide earth, whose end is very far away, in this Yajña. Those lucky and victorious ones hold everything. May heaven and earth protect us from sin.

8. If we have sinned against gods, or friends, or the lord of everything born, may our intelligence be able to destroy these sins. May heaven and earth protect us from sin.

9. May both, worthy of praise by men, protect me. May both provide us with means of protection. O gods, we noble ones desire plenty of wealth to live happily and donate generously.

10. I, of good intellect, speak that first truth for earth and heaven. Those two living near protect us from sins. Protect us like mother and father.

11. Mother earth and father heaven, what I ask for you here, let that become true. Become the protector of gods. Let us receive food, strength and long life.

While most often earth is considered the mother and heaven the father, this representation is not unique. In verse five, both earth and heaven are considered ladies, and God is considered the father of both. In verse seven the ends of earth are considered very far and Yajña takes place at the ends. The ends are very far away, because observer space spans across the whole universe, and at the boundary of the universe the creation of matter and energy takes place, which is called Yajña. The transformation of matter into energy is related to the concept of the immortality of the gods in the Vedas.

“We are like butterflies who flutter for a day and think it is forever.”
– Carl Sagan

7. THE SEAT OF IMMORTALITY

Once you realize what Pṛthivī, Antarikṣa and Dyau stand for, your immediate concern will be to know what their most distinguishing features are. Pṛthivī is considered “Martyaloka” in Hindu scriptures, meaning where life has a limited span and death cannot be avoided.

“Immortals purified three brilliant forms of Agni. Out of them one who eats was placed where death is inevitable, other two went in sibling Lokas.” Ṛgveda 3.2.9

In this verse Pṛthivī and other two spaces are described as siblings. Modern physics tells us about the cosmic dance of particles. Everywhere in the universe particles are being created and annihilated continuously. These particles have a lifespan between the creation and annihilation. In Vedas Pṛthivī is the abode of particles, which are created and annihilated. These particles are given the name “Janāḥ” meaning people because they live and die like people. Vedās talk about five types of particles again and again and give them the name “Pañcajanāḥ” meaning five people. The system of four Varṇas was a social order consisting of Brāhmaṇa, Kṣatriya, Vaiśya and Śūdra. Five people refer to five types of particles, and commentators not knowing this difference often describe five people as Brāhmaṇa, Ksatriya, Vaiśya, Śūdra and Niṣāda (fisherman). This makes no sense as fisherman obviously belongs to Śūdra category and cannot be counted separately. Dyau is the abode of energy. Energy is not created and annihilated like particles, therefore energy can be considered eternal or immortal. Once Dyau became heaven, and various forms of energy became gods, gods became immortal in their heavenly abode. Vedas frequently describe gods as being immortal meaning that energy is eternal. Yajurveda 32.10 says that in the third abode immortal gods live. The third abode is heaven or the light space.

7.1: The wedding of Vivasvāna

The concept of hidden space has been elaborated in the Vedas by various examples. The Vedas talk about the same phenomenon in various ways. The tale of Vivasvāna and Saraṇyū is told to illustrate the formation of three spaces.

"Tvaṣṭā is about to perform the marriage ceremony of his daughter and this whole universe has come to attend. Mother of Yama was married, great wife of Vivasvāna disappeared." Ṛgveda 10.17.1

"Immortal was hidden for mortals, similar lady was made and given to Vivasvāna. Saraṇyū was there and she conceived two Aśvins. She gave birth to twins (Yama and Yamī). Ṛgveda 10.17.2

These two verses describe the early universe, when the universe is divided in three spaces. Vivasvāna is the observer space and Saraṇyū is light space during this period. Saraṇyū means quickly moving, which is apt name considering that light propagates in that space. Disappearance of Saraṇyū is the concealment of light space. Second verse makes the point clear where Saraṇyū is considered immortal. So who is the replacement of Saraṇyū? No name is given, but intermediate space fits the description very well. The presence of Saraṇyū in a hidden form matches very well with the concept of three spaces, and finally two very mysterious verses make sense.

There is a Greek myth related to these verses. Zeus was unfaithful to his wife Hera on several occasions. Hera left Zeus due to his romantic adventures and went to a place called Euboea. Zeus asked Cithaeron for advice, who suggested that he perform a sham marriage. A wooden image of Plataea, daughter of Asopus, was made and Zeus performed the drama of marrying her. Hera heard of this and came to the scene. She tore the bridal veil and discovered the wooden image behind it. After knowing the truth she started living with Zeus again.

Saraṇyū is the mother of two Aśvins, but why are they called Aśvins? Aśvin is made from the word "Aśva" meaning horse. The Brāhmaṇa texts have come up with a story as an explanation. The Śatapatha Brāhmaṇa tells that Saraṇyū assumed the form of a mare. Vivasvāna took the form of a horse and mated with her. From their intercourse two Aśvins were born. Again there is an exact Greek counterpart of this myth. Demeter Erinnys assumed the form of a mare and was pursued by Poseidon in the form of a stallion. Demeter was worshipped in the form of a woman with mare's head. This myth is not found in the Vedas and proves that the Greek civilization is post-brāhmaṇic.

7.2: The field

Now we know that the observer space is the abode of matter particles, and the light space is the abode of energy. The question now is what is the significance of intermediate space? The intermediate space (Antarikṣa) is the abode of field. The principal deity of Antarikṣa is Vāyu.

"Vāyu brightens in Antarikṣa." Jaimini Brāhmaṇa 1.192

Vāyu being the deity of Antarikṣa, and Antarikṣa being in between Pṛthivī and Dyau, it makes perfect sense that universe was divided in two by Vāyu (Vāyu Purāṇa 24.74). There are four complete hymns dedicated to Vāyu in the Ṛgveda (1.134, 4.48, 10.168, 10.186). The meaning of Vāyu is made clear by the following mantra.

"The sun and the rest of the universe are woven in a string. What is that string that is Vāyu." Śatapatha Brāhmaṇa 8.7.3.10

Apparent meaning of Vāyu is air. This verse clearly shows that here Vāyu cannot mean air. In fact there cannot be a better definition of the scientific term "field". Thus Pṛthivī, Antarikṣa and Dyau are the abodes of matter particles, field and energy respectively. Field is another form of energy, and therefore Yajurveda says:

"Vāyu has penetrating brightness." Yajurveda 1.24

7.3: Fabric of the universe

If the space is an aggregate of three intertwined spaces, out of which we can observe only one directly, our space will seem to us as having holes, as if part of it is missing. This is the realm of quantum physics, where particles seem to be taking quantum jumps, not moving continuously, because fabric of the universe is perforated. These holes are referred to in a verse in Yajurveda.

"May Pṛthivī, Vāyu and Dyau complete your holes." Yajurveda 23.43

Here Vāyu represents intermediate space (Antarikṣa), as Vāyu is the principal deity of Antarikṣa. Observer space (Pṛthivī), intermediate space (Antarikṣa) and light space (Dyau) each are perforated, only all three together make the space complete without holes. According to Vedas, earth and heaven were together initially and they were separated later by Vāyu. These ideas traveled very widely all over the world.

7.4: Heaven and Earth

Pṛthivī is considered the mother and Dyau is considered the father in the Vedas, and they form a pair Dyāvāpṛthivī together. One of the most beautiful verses of the Ṛgveda says:

"Heaven is my father, brother atmosphere is my navel, and great earth is my mother." Ṛgveda 1.164.33

Another verse from Atharvaveda says:

"This land is my mother. I am the son of earth." Atharvaveda 12.1.12

In their apparent meaning earth and heaven do not look like a pair as earth is negligibly small compared to heaven. In their scientific meaning as observer and light spaces, the description of them as a pair looks perfect. In the Vedas Pṛthivī cannot mean earth for the simple reason that the Vedas talk of three Pṛthivīs, while there could not be more than one earth.

"Ādityas hold three earths and three heavens." Ṛgveda 2.27.8

"Agni is established in first, second and third earth." Yajurveda 5.9

The division of universe in three spaces is at a very subtle level far beyond the capabilities of modern science to observe it, but Vedic scientists divided even that length in three, calling them upper, medium and lower. The story of the division of universe in earth and heaven was very well known in ancient world, but their scientific meaning was known only to few people outside India. These ideas were picked up by Semitic religions, without having the slightest clue as to their scientific meaning. Bible, Genesis 1.1 says that God created the heaven and the earth in the beginning. Koran 21.30 talks about the division of the universe in earth and heaven. In Greek mythology, in the beginning there was Chaos, a swirling formless mass, from which came Gaia, mother earth, and her consort Uranus, the heaven. In Egypt, Seb (earth) and Nut (heaven) formed a pair, from whom many gods were born. In Chinese creation myths an egg arises in emptiness. Pangu, the first god, was residing in the egg. Universe was divided in heaven (yang) and earth (yin), when the egg broke. Pangu held the heavens, so that earth would not be crushed. Pangu grew by ten feet every day, and he died after 10,000 years. Animals and other features of earth were made from Pangu's body. Yang is considered male and yin is considered female in Chinese myths. Maori tribes of New Zealand also believed in a divine pair Rangi (heaven) and Papa (earth). Mangaians and Samoans of South Pacific along with Maoris of New Zealand and Acagchemem natives in California held that heaven and earth were touching in the beginning and were pushed apart later. Among Greeks, Ouranos does the job of separating earth from heaven, while in Mangaians, god Ru does this work. Among Maoris, Tutenganahau pushes earth and heaven apart. These ideas are Vedic ideas dispersed among inhabitants all around the globe. The world has completely forgotten where these ideas came from, because it happened a very long time ago during the dawn of human civilization.

7.5: The cosmic tree

Figure 7.1 shows a tree with two animal heads joined to it. These two animals are heaven and earth depicted according to the following verse in the Vedas:

"Which is that tree from which earth and heaven have been formed? O wise people, ask about that which is holding the whole universe." Ṛgveda 10.81.4, Yajurveda 17.20

Figure 7.1: Earth and heaven represented as animal heads coming out of a fig tree, a seal from Indus Valley (Marshal: Plate XC)

In another verse mother earth and father heaven are described playing on a tree (Yajurveda 23.25). Analogy of God with a tree is well accepted in the Vedic literature. The Śvetāśvatar Upaniṣad says:

"There is nothing beyond him, nothing smaller or bigger. He is the one staying in heaven like a tree. All this is created by complete Puruṣa." Śvetāśvatar Upaniṣad 3.9

The tree chosen for this representation was sacred fig tree, called Aśvattha in Sanskrit and now popularly known as the Pīpala tree.

7.6: The giant tortoise

One popular Hindu myth says that earth rests on the back of a giant tortoise. Another popular myth says that earth rests on the head of a serpent, Śeṣanāga. Earthquakes are supposed to take place when the tortoise or the serpent moves. The origin of the serpent myth is the story of serpent Vṛtra. We will trace here the origin of the tortoise myth. Like most of the beliefs of the Hindus, the origin of this myth can also be traced to the Vedas. The Vedas tell us the following:

"Heaven is fierce and earth is firm due to him." Ṛgveda 10.121.5, Yajurveda 32.6

We should note here that firm here is used in the sense of being very hard and not as stationary. Heaven (Dyau) is fierce because it is the abode of energy and earth (Pṛthivī) is firm because it is the abode of particles which do not have wave like characteristics. Pṛthivī is considered like a tortoise in Vedic scriptures. Tortoise has a very firm back without any hair on it. Observer space (Pṛthivī) is firm like the back of tortoise and it does not have hair as well.

"This Pṛthivī was without hair earlier." Śatpatha Brāhmaṇa 2.2.4.3, Aitareya Brāhmaṇa 24.22

"This Pṛthivī is like the back of the tortoise." Mahābhārata, Śāntiparva 300.6

Hair refers to the field lines. Even modern physicists use similar analogy when they say that black holes do not have hair meaning that field lines cannot emerge from a black hole. Pṛthivī does not have hair, because hair is a characteristic of the field, and the field resides in Antarikṣa. The Vedic ideas were picked up by the Semitic religions without having any clue as to the real scientific meaning behind these ideas. The Bible also says that earth was bald earlier in Genesis. In India massive efforts were made to preserve the scientific meaning of the Vedas. Still, the analogy between Pṛthivī and the back of the tortoise was forgotten long time back, and then a myth generated which supposes that earth rests on the back of a giant tortoise and earthquakes take place when the tortoise turns.

7.7: The geocentric universe

The firmness of earth is referred several times in Bible, where firmness has been associated with immovability. In Psalm 93:1, Psalm 96.10 and 104:5 it is said that earth has been fixed on its foundation and cannot be moved. The concept of the firmness of observer space (earth) gave rise to the concept of immovability of earth in Semitic religions and formed the basis of the geocentric universe. In ancient and medieval times ideas after ideas originated from India and some of them were incorporated in the belief system of Semitic religions. According to the Bible and the Koran earth was created before sun. This is the result of confusion that took place in India as the Vedic knowledge was forgotten.

As the observer space and light space were separated in the very beginning of creation, it is very difficult to know how the process of separation started.

"Which was born first and which later? How were they born? Who knows?" Ṛgveda 1.185.1

Ṛgveda 10.81.3 clearly states that both of them were born together, but later scriptures seem to be of the opinion that observer space was created first.

"This Pṛthivī was born first among the Bhutas." Śatpatha Brāhmaṇa 14.1.2.10

"This Pṛthivī was first created among the Lokas." Śatapatha Brāhmaṇa 6.5.3.1

In the Śatapatha Brāhmaṇa we see Pṛthivī counted among three spaces (lokas), and as well as among five elements (Bhutas). Confusion of Pṛthivī with earth resulted in the belief that earth was older than sun, as sun is part of heaven. Pṛthivī was not hard when it was created according to Hindu scriptures. Earlier it was very soft, which gradually hardened.

7.8: Superspace

Beginning of this century saw the rise of theory of relativity. Earlier scientists considered space and time as independent of each other. Theory of relativity gave rise to the concept of the four dimensional space-time, in which space has three dimensions and time has one dimension. Although mathematically it is easy to incorporate time as one more dimension to space, physically it is not so easy to conceptualize. Though flow of time is affected by the curvature of space, is it strong enough evidence to think of time as similar to space? We can move forward and backward in space, but we cannot move backward in time, and we can move forward in time only at a fixed rate. Why this should be so in a four-dimensional universe is not satisfactorily explained by modern physics.

Once the concept of four-dimensional universe gained ground, scientists tried to further expand it. One of the major triumphs of general theory of relativity was that it explained gravitation as the interaction of matter with the curvature of space-time. Soon scientists started to generalize the idea and proposed a universe of even higher dimensions in order to explain the electromagnetic force as another manifestation of the properties of space-time. These universes of higher assumed dimensions are called Superspaces. With the discovery of nuclear forces the number of dimensions needed to accommodate these forces also increased. The theory of Superspaces has not been perfected yet. The reason being that it is not easy to verify these theories. They propose more than one dimensions of time, physical meaning of which is unclear. If there are more than four dimensions then why do not we observe them? Scientists believe that some of the dimensions are curled at a very subtle level. If you look at a cylinder, which has two dimensions, from far away, it looks like a line, which has only one dimension. Thus universe could have more dimensions than we are actually aware of. Sylvester James Gates, String theorist at University of Maryland says that those other dimensions are curled up so tight, we'll never have to deal with them. Scientists have found that in order for Superspace theories to work, these spaces must have at least ten dimensions. We should recall that according to the Ṛgveda, the outside of universe is ten-dimensional. Clearly, universe is a Superspace in the framework of the Vedic cosmology. The Vedas imagine the inside of the universe to be different than outside. Inside of the universe is divided in observer, intermediate and light spaces, each of which has only seven dimensions.

"Seven were its enclosures (Paridhi), three times seven were made firelogs (Samidha)." Ṛgveda 10.90.15

Here seven firelogs refer to seven dimensions each of the three spaces. Seven enclosures refer to curled dimensions. Vedic scientists had a clear conception of the geometry of the universe, and therefore we find exact numbers in Vedas. The meaning of all these numbers is not clear to me at the present time. What is clear is that the Vedas form the basis of Hindu way of life. The science of Vedas has been incorporated in Hindu customs, so that Hindus do not forget the science behind. One of the most beautiful expressions of Vedic science is the custom of going round the fire seven times by the bride and groom during marriage ceremony. In Vedic science the dimensions are called firelogs, meaning energy resides in them. The seven rounds around fire represent the seven curled dimensions. We have a reference to curled dimensions in following mantra.

"Directions are enclosed meters." Śatapatha Brāhmaṇa 8.5.2.3

There are seven prominent metres and in this mantra they are related to the seven dimensions of the observer space. The Vedas consider dimensions to exist inside and outside the universe, and also consider the dimensions to have magnetic properties.

"Directions are inside the universe and outside as well." Śatapatha Brāhmaṇa 6.5.2.7

"Directions have properties of iron." Śatapatha Brāhmaṇa 13.2.10.3

Here by iron, magnetic properties are meant. We should note that apparent meaning of these mantras make no sense at all. Once we know the scientific meaning of these mantras, then these mantras reveal the mind boggling achievements of the Vedic sages.

7.9: Triśirā Viśvarūpa

One of the legendary deeds of Indra is the slaying of Viśvarūpa, son of Tvaṣṭā. Following two verses from the Ṛgveda describe this legend.

"Instigated by Indra, he Āptya (Trita), knowledgeable of forefather's weaponry, fought for long period. Trita killed the three-headed with seven rays, and obtained the cows of Tvaṣṭā's son." Ṛgveda 10.8.8

"Indra, protector of truthful people, shattered very strong and haughty. He, calling the cows, cut three heads of Tvaṣṭā's son Viśvarūpa." Ṛgveda 10.8.9

Triśirā means three-headed and Viśvarūpa means shape of the universe. Three heads of the universe are the end points of Pṛthivī, Antarikṣa and Dyau. As these three spaces exist at every point in the universe, these three exist at the boundary of the universe as well. Thus killing of Triśirā Viśvarūpa is the same as that of killing of Vṛtra, and both represent the expansion of the universe. Seven rays of Triśirā Viśvarūpa are the seven dimensions of the universe. Figure 7.2 shows Triśirā Viśvarūpa as found on a seal in Indus Valley Civilization. Some scholars have tried to explain the three heads of the animal as only one head in three different positions. This explanation is the result of their unfamiliarity with the Ṛgveda or their prejudice in considering the Indus Valley people different from the Vedic people.

In Aitareya Brāhmaṇa, Indra kills three-headed son of Tvaṣṭā named Vairūpa. Vairūpa was considered a Brāhmaṇa, and Indra commits a grave sin by killing him, so that he had to atone for it. A parallel myth is found among Greeks as well. Apollo also commits a sin by slaying Pytho the dragon and had to be purified. What is important is that this story of atonement is not found in the Vedas.

Figure 7.2: Triśirā Viśvarūpa, a seal from Indus Valley (Marshal: Plate CXII)

Thus Greeks borrowed their myths not from the Vedas, but from the Brāhmaṇas which has been written and spread all around the globe before the Greek Civilization came into being.

7.10: The Dark Matter

One of the key features of the Big Bang Cosmology is the dark matter. The universe is supposed to have a theoretical mass-energy density in order to have existed for so long, and on the other hand observed mass-energy density is far lower than that. Most observations put the observed density at 10 % of theoretical density. So what happened to 90 % of the mass-energy that should be there, but is not really there? Scientists have given this missing mass-energy the name dark matter. At present scientists have no clue as to what could be the dark matter.

One popular theory is that the dark matter consists of massive neutrinos. The neutrinos that scientists are familiar with have no mass or very small mass. On the other hand dark matter has to be taken into account, as its gravitational pull affects the evolution of the universe. The Vedic sages were also very familiar with the concept of dark matter. The Ṛgveda talks about the dark matter in following verses:

"All that is born, is his one fourth, his three fourth is immortal in heaven." Ṛgveda 10.90.3

"Three-fourth of Puruṣa is above, his one fourth is born again and again." Ṛgveda 10.90.4

"Speech has four quarters, which knowledgeable people know. Three of them are hidden and not known by people. People speak only the fourth one." Ṛgveda 1.164.45

First two verses establish that only 25 % of mass-energy is located in observer space, while 75 % of mass-energy is located in light space. Our measurements can reach only 25 % of the total mass-energy of the universe. It is this 25 % of mass-energy that keeps being created and annihilated as particles in observer space. The third verse refers to the same phenomenon, however it gives the name speech to the mass-energy of the universe. The Vedas talk about same phenomenon in various forms as illustrations so that key concepts are not forgotten. It is very clear that the Vedas consider 75 % of the mass-energy of the universe to be located in light space in the form of pure energy. In Hindu scriptures earth and heaven together with fire, air and water form the five elements from which everything in the universe is made. As modern science has shown, the idea of these five elements constituting the universe is very primitive. Now that we know the real scientific meaning of some of these elements, we are in a position to appreciate the thinking of the Vedic sages. We will now discuss in more detail the scientific meaning of the rest of the elements, and find out that the ingredients of everything in the universe are indeed five elements.

"The essential reality is a set of fields."
- Steven Weinberg

8. RETURN OF THE ELEMENTS

In ancient India concept of five elements was very well known. These five elements were earth, water, sky, fire and air. Greeks borrowed this concept from India, but they considered only four elements leaving out the sky element. The concept of sky as an element must have been considered very abstruse by Greeks. The actual scientific meaning of these five elements was quite different from their apparent meaning. These five elements in technical terms are Pṛthivī (earth), Āpaḥ (water), Dyau (sky), Agni (Fire) and Vāyu (air). We have already met three of these elements, Pṛthivī, Dyau and Vāyu in the previous chapter. We will focus our discussion to the meaning of Agni and Āpaḥ now.

8.1: Agni (Fire)

Agni means one that leads. Related word "Agra" in Sanskrit means front. Agni is the most important diety after Indra in the Ṛgveda. All books except one in the Ṛgveda start with hymns dedicated to Agni. Sanskrit Agni became Ignis in Latin, Ugnis in Lithuanian and Ogni in Slevanic. Agni in scientific terminology is "Energy". In Ṛgveda 2.10.6 Agni is called full of honey. The meaning of this mysterious verse will become clear, when we discuss honey later in this book. Agni is described as having three forms in the Ṛgveda, and sometimes the other two forms are called brothers of Agni.

"Immortals purified three brilliant forms of Agni. Out of them one who eats was placed where death is inevitable, other two went in sibling spaces." Ṛgveda 3.2.9

These three forms are Agni, Vāyu and Sūrya. The division of universe in three spaces is the basis for three forms of Agni. Agni is called Agni in observer space, and this is the space where matter particles take birth and die. Agni is called Vāyu (field) in intermediate space, and field is only another form of energy. Agni is called Sūrya in light space.

8.2: Āpaḥ (Water)

Āpaḥ means what pervades, and if there is any confusion as to the extent of this pervasion, the Ṛgveda clears this confusion in the following mantra:

"Waters pervade the whole universe, which holds fire in its womb. There exists the one lord of all gods, for which god should we offer oblation." Ṛgveda 10.121.7

"Āpaḥ held universe in its womb" Ṛgveda 10.82.6

Āpaḥ are everywhere in the world, and there is Agni residing in the Āpah. As Agni has been identified with energy, Āpaḥ is certainly manifestation of energy. To get further insight in the concept of Āpaḥ, it is time to recall a mantra from the Śatapatha Brāhmaṇa.

"Āpaḥ were indeed Salila earlier." Śatapatha Brāhmaṇa 11.1.6.1

Salila has been identified with undifferentiated primordial fluid. So what happens when the undifferentiated gets differentiated? There is a polarization and formation of opposites. Scientifically Āpaḥ is the soup of matter-antimatter particles that pervades the universe. Matter and antimatter can be considered polarization of energy. When a particle meets its anti-particle, it changes into energy. Once Āpaḥ is identified with matter and anti-matter, energy (Agni) clearly resides in it, and a great Vedic puzzle has been solved. Vedas repeatedly mention fire residing in waters, which apparently makes no sense as water is used to quench fire. Now is the perfect time to read a beautiful hymn dedicated to goddess Āpaḥ.

Ṛgveda 7.49

Sage: Maitrāvaruṇi Vasiṣṭha; Deity: Āpaḥ; Metre: Triṣṭupa

1. From the middle of Salila, great among seas, purifying Āpaḥ keep flowing without resting for a moment. Whom bull Indra, who holds Vajra, dug to flow, goddess Āpaḥ help me here.

2. Those from heaven or those which flow, those from well or those self-born, those purifying Āpaḥ going to sea, goddess Āpaḥ help me here.

3. Whose king Varuṇa moves in the middle observing the truth and lies of people, which drips honey, which is clean and pure, goddess Āpaḥ help me here.

4. In which king Varuṇa and Soma are, where all the gods get their energy, in which Vaiśvānara Agni has entered, goddess Āpaḥ help me here.

In these verses a clear relationship is made between Āpah and Indra, Varuṇa, Agni and Soma. We are now in position to understand the relationship between Āpah, Indra and Agni, and meaning of the rest of the relationship will become clear when I discuss Varuṇa and Soma.

The Padma Purāṇa in twenty fifth chapter of the creation canto tells the following story about the dwarf incarnation described earlier. Daitya (demon) Vāṣkali became very powerful because of a boon given by Brahmā. Indra asked for land from Asuras and said: "Brāhmaṇa (Viṣṇu) is born in the lineage of Kaśyapa. He asked me for land equal to three steps, but I do not have anything. Please fulfill his desire." Vāṣkali's priest Śukrāchārya tried to stop him, but Vāṣkali agreed anyway as there was a custom to never let a Brāhmaṇa return empty-handed. Viṣṇu put one step in Sūrya (sun) loka, another in Dhruva (fixed) loka, and with his third step he hit the cover of the universe. A hole developed in the cover and a profuse amount of water gushed in the universe from outside. This water took the form of Gaṅgā (Ganges) river and therefore is famous in the world as Viṣṇupadī, meaning born out of the feet of Lord Viṣṇu. This concept of water gushing in from the outside of universe has been borrowed by Semitic religions. The Bible (Genesis 7:11-12, 8:2 and Malachi 3:10) talks about the windows of heaven, which God opens to let the water from outside gush in.

The water that Hindu scriptures refer to is not water, but matter and antimatter that constitute the universe. The hole in the cover of the universe refers to the surface of the universe being broken by the expansion of the universe. According to Hindu scriptures when the water from outside gushes into the universe, it takes the form of the Gaṅgā river, which falls on the lock of hair of Lord Śiva, and then is transferred to earth. For this reason Gaṅgā river is represented as coming out of the lock of hair of Lord Śiva. To understand the science behind this representation, we have to discuss the Ṛgvedic form of Lord Śiva, that is Rudra.

8.3: Rudra

There are three complete hymns dedicated to Rudra in the Ṛgveda (1.114, 2.33 and 7.46). As the universe expands, matter-antimatter is created at the surface of the universe. The matter-antimatter then starts to travel inside the universe. However matter and antimatter cannot continue their journey, as they annihilate each other. As matter and antimatter annihilate each other, they change into radiation. This radiation is called Rudra by Vedic scientists. Rudra means what makes one cry, which refers to the penetrating brightness of radiation. Earth and heaven together are called Rodasī, meaning crying, referring to their being filled up with radiation.

The concept of the Vedic god Rudra later developed in the form of Lord Śiva in the Purāṇas. Śiva is considered the god of annihilation, which is only appropriate. When particles are annihilated, they change into radiation. The lock of hair of Lord Śiva is Vāyu, as Vāyu consists of field lines. Lord Śiva is very kind, but at times he becomes very furious. He has similar attributes in the Vedas. Radiation can be soothing or penetrating depending on intensity. In the Ṛgveda Rudra is sometimes used in singular case and sometimes in plural case. It seems that the Vedic sages divided radiation in various categories depending on intensity, and used singular case when considering radiation as a whole or used plural case when considering differing intensities of radiation. Bow and arrow is the weapon of Rudra in the Ṛgveda. In the Yajurveda, the character of Rudra develops further. Sixteenth chapter of the Yajurveda is called Rudrādhyāya, and contains beautiful description of Rudra. He is called Śambhu, Śaṅkara and Śiva, the names by which he is known today. In the Ṛgveda Rudra is not shown assisting Indra, and therefore the proponents of the Aryan Invasion Theory claim that Rudra was a Dravidian god. They conveniently conceal that in the Ṛgveda sons of Rudra, Marutas, are described helping Indra.

8.4: Maruta (wind)

There are twenty nine complete hymns dedicated to Marutas in the Ṛgveda (1.37-39, 1.64, 1.85-88, 1.166, 1.168, 1.172, 2.34, 5.52-59, 6.66, 7.56-58, 8.7, 8.20, 8.94, and 10.77-78). Marutas (winds) are called the sons of Rudra (Ṛgveda 1.64.12). Marutas are seen as helping Indra in slaying of Vṛtra (Ṛgveda 1.165.7). You have already seen that slaying of Vṛtra is the expansion of the universe. What role do Maruta have to play in this expansion? I will illustrate this point with the example of a balloon. Consider the balloon as representing the universe, and we are considering here the entire balloon not just the surface. To expand the balloon, you blow air into it. What does the air do? It increases the pressure inside which expands the balloon. Now consider the universe which is being filled by radiation as matter and antimatter annihilate each other. This radiation creates a pressure, radiation pressure, and this radiation pressure expands the universe. I will identify Maruta as radiation pressure. As Rudra is radiation, and radiation pressure (Maruta) results due to radiation, it is only appropriate to call Maruta sons of Rudra.

Pressure has a very important property. At any point in space, pressure is same in all directions. Pressure is a tensor quantity like stress. In a three-dimensional space, stress has nine components. Nine components arise by squaring of three, the number of dimensions in space. If we have a higher dimensional space, number of components of stress will simply be square of the number of dimensions. We have already seen that Vedic scientists consider inside of the universe to be of seven dimensions, and therefore pressure will have seven cross seven, forty nine components. This is exactly the number of Maruta, forty nine, and they are also supposed to move in seven rows, each row having seven Marutas (Ṛgveda 5.52.17). The Ṛgveda contains a beautiful dialogue between Indra and Marutas. Indra sees the Marutas and says few words in their praise. Marutas become haughty to hear that and despise Indra. This makes Indra furious and he starts describing his glories. Finally Marutas relent, and accept the superiority of Indra. Indra and Marutas then resume their friendship.

Ṛgveda 1.165

Sage: 1, 2, 4, 6, 8, 10, 11, 12 – Indra, 3, 5, 7, 9 – Maruta;

Deity: Marutwānindra; Meter: Triṣṭupa

1. Indra: Having same age and same abode, equal in all respect, with which auspicious brilliance do Marutas sprinkle together? What is their desire? Where do they come from? Rain producing Marutas worship strength to acquire wealth.
2. Indra: Whose hymns of praises do the young ones enjoy. Who turns in non-violent sacrifice? With which great thoughts can I make them happy who move in atmosphere like eagles?
3. Maruta: O Indra, where do you go alone even though you are great? O protector of truthful people, why are you in such a condition? Walking together we ask you, owner of horses, whatever you want to say, say to us in beautiful words.
4. Indra: Praises, thoughts and Soma provide me happiness. My strength is well known. Praises come to me. Let my two horses take me there directly.
5. Maruta: Therefore we have adorned our bodies with our strength, and joined with near ones. We have come to you. O Indra, make your strength favorable to us.
6. Indra: O Marutas, where was your strength, when I was left alone to slay the serpent. I am fierce, strong and great. I have killed all the enemies.

7. Maruta: O Bull, you have performed many great deeds, but we have also contributed to that by joining forces with you. O mighty Indra, we have also done many great acts. Marutas work to get what they desire.
8. Indra: O Marutas, I killed Vṛtra and became strong on my own. I hold Vajra in my hand. I have created the flowing waters, which give happiness to all.
9. Maruta: O Maghavan (wealthy), there is nothing that has not been instigated by you. There is no other learned god like you. O great Indra, the deeds you have performed and will perform, neither anyone else has done it nor will be born to do it.
10. Indra: Whatever I want to do, I put my mind into it. The vigor of me alone spreads in all directions. O Marutas, I am fierce and learned. Wherever I go, I become the lord of that place.
11. Indra: O friend Marutas, the praises you made for me here have made me very happy. You have strengthened my body by your bodies. You have done it for rain producer, sacrifice performer Indra.
12. Indra: O Marutas, be friendly to me the same way. Hold praiseworthy wealth and food. Aim for me and cover me with glory, O beautiful Marutas.

All Maruta are of same age, none of them is younger or older (Verse one). We immediately recognize that this refers to pressure being same in all directions. Marutas belong to intermediate space (Verse two). Maruta and Vāyu both are synonyms, and it is only expected that they will belong to intermediate space. Indra killed the serpent alone (Verse six). This refers to the initial moments of creation. As there was very little matter and energy in the universe then, electric force alone was responsible for expansion of the universe. Once universe had sufficient matter and energy, then Marutas joined hands with Indra to expand the universe. Marutas wear gold ornaments on their chests (Ṛgveda 5.55.1, 5.57.5). This refers to Marutas carrying energy with them. In the Ṛgveda characters of Maruta and Vāyu are very distinct. Vāyu has neither been called son of Rudra nor told to be more than one. The Ṛgveda is a book of science, and once we understand this, then we will see clearly that different terms in the Ṛgveda have different scientific meanings. The Ṛgveda is a coded book, and water of the Ṛgveda does not mean water and rivers of the Ṛgveda do not carry water. Most prominent river in the Ṛgveda is Saraswatī, and it is time to discuss the concept of Saraswatī in greater detail.

8.5: Saraswatī

Two complete hymns have been dedicated to Saraswatī in the Ṛgveda (7.95 and 7.96). Saraswatī has been worshipped as the goddess of learning in India. Saraswatī was also a mighty river in India during the Vedic age, which dried up later. How did Saraswatī become associated with speech and river, two widely different concepts? The answer lies in the scientific symbolism of the Ṛgveda, where hardly any word means what it is supposed to mean if you consider the apparent (ruḍhi) meaning of the word. On the other hand, every word in the Ṛgveda means exactly what it is supposed to mean, if you consider the etymological (yaugika) meaning of the word. Speech (Vāk) is considered sacred in India and is another form of God. The Ṛgveda itself attests to the equivalence of speech and God in the following verses:

"All that is born, is his one fourth, his three fourth is immortal in heaven." Ṛgveda 10.90.3

"Three-fourth of Puruṣa is above, his one fourth is born again and again." Ṛgveda 10.90.4

"Speech has four quarters, which knowledgeable people know. Three of them are hidden and not known by people. People speak only the fourth one." Ṛgveda 1.164.45

The equivalence of Speech and God is described in Bible as well. Is it any wonder that Speech says the following about herself in Ṛgveda 10.125.1.

"I walk with Rudras and Vasus. I live with Ādityas and all the gods. I hold Mitra and Varuṇa. I hold Indra, Agni and both Aśvins."

Saraswatī became the goddess of learning because of her association with Speech. Brāhmaṇa texts emphasize this aspect again and again.

"Speech is Saraswatī." Śatpatha Brāhmaṇa 2.5.4.6, 3.1.4.9, 4.2.5.14, Taittirīya Brāhmaṇa 1.3.4.5, 3.8.11.2, Aitareya Brāhmaṇa 2.24

Ilā, Saraswatī and Bhāratī form a triad in the Ṛgveda. Sāyaṇa in his commentary on Ṛgveda 1.142.9 places Ilā in Pṛthivī, Saraswatī in Antarikṣa and Bhāratī in Dyau. This view is further supported by the Ṛgveda itself. In verse 2.30.8 Saraswatī is asked to join with Marutas, and Marutas belong to intermediate space. In verse 7.96.2 Saraswatī is called friend of Marutas. Pururavā is called son of Ilā in Ṛgveda 10.95.18, and in the same hymn Pururavā is depicted as a mortal. Death of particles takes place in observer space, so Ilā belongs to Pṛthivī. Thus speech (Vāk) is the total mass-energy of the universe, and Ilā, Saraswatī and Bhāratī are the respective portions of mass-energy in the observer, intermediate and light spaces.

There is one important point to be discussed here. Space is divided in three, and these three spaces have different volumes, intermediate space having the smallest volume as it is only an interface between the observer and light spaces. Another way of division is not according to volume, but content. Observer and light spaces may have same volume, but there mass-energy contents may be vastly different. Confusion arises when these two different concepts are equated. Speech has traditionally been divided in three categories: Paśyantī representing Bhāratī, Madhyamā representing Saraswatī, and Vaikharī representing Ilā. Madhyamā means intermediate, and thus Saraswatī belonging to intermediate space gets further support. However, in Ṛgveda 1.164.45 quoted above, Speech is said to have four quarters, and confusion runs amok. Sāyaṇa in his commentary on this verse adds another form of speech called "Parā" and brings the total to four. Speech (Vāk) of Ṛgveda has nothing to do with speech, as it represents the total mass-energy of the universe. Verses 10.90.3-4 and 1.164.45 are saying that 75 % of total mass-energy is in the light space and only 25 % is in the observer space. In this consideration, intermediate space becomes part of light space, as both of them are hidden. Intermediate space being only an interface, counting of it as a separate phase is optional. When the Ṛgveda talks about this four-fold division, it is based on content, and when Ṛgveda talks about three-fold division it is based on extent.

Saraswatī has been called fortress of iron in Ṛgveda 7.95.1. This description neither fits Saraswatī as speech nor fits Saraswatī as a river. Some western scholars like Max Müler justify this epithet by saying that wide river Saraswatī protected India from invasion. However, this justification does not fit well with facts. Western boundary of India has traditionally been Indus river and not Saraswatī. A large number of cities belonging to Indus Valley Civilization have existed on both sides of Saraswatī. Thus Saraswatī could have nourished Vedic civilization, but not protected it. The scientific explanation is that iron represents magnetism everywhere in the Ṛgveda, and as Saraswatī represents the flow of matter and energy, it has magnetic properties.

Now that the relationship of Saraswatī with Speech is clear, it is time to discuss the relationship of Saraswatī with river. Saraswatī has been called as one having seven sisters in Ṛgveda 6.61.10. These seven sisters are commonly counted as seven rivers of northern India and Pakistan. However, there are so many rivers in this region, and why would only seven be chosen? Number seven has a special significance in the Ṛgveda as in seven sages, seven enclosures, seven meters, seven times seven Marutas and so on. This will be too much of a coincidence, if there are exactly seven rivers as well. Sāyaṇa gives a clue when he says that Gāyatrī etc. meters are seven sisters, and similar to them Gaṃgā etc. seven rivers are seven sisters. Thus seven sisters of Saraswatī are seven dimensions of intermediate space. It is for this reason that Saraswatī makes a triad with Ilā and Bhāratī on one hand, and makes a group of seven rivers with Gaṃgā, Indus and other rivers on the other hand. Universe has three spaces and each space has seven dimensions, and Saraswatī forms a group of three or seven corresponding to the number of spaces or dimensions.

In the Ṛgveda Saraswatī is not a river carrying water. The Ṛgveda uses objects familiar to the Vedic people, and uses them in an entirely different context. There is little doubt that a river named Saraswatī existed during Vedic times, but to try to get further information about river Saraswatī from the Ṛgveda is a futile exercise. What the Ṛgveda has to say about Saraswatī can never apply to a river. In Ṛgveda 7.95.2 Saraswatī is said to flow from ocean. The word used is "Samudrāt" meaning from ocean, and not into. No river on earth does that. Also, Saraswatī is well accepted to belong to intermediate space, so she does not flow on earth at all. The rivers of the Ṛgveda are not rivers of water. Matter and energy are created at the boundary of the universe, and start their journey towards the center of the universe. This flow of matter and energy is termed river in the Ṛgveda. This representation fits well with the code of the Ṛgveda, as Āpah (water) of Ṛgveda is in fact matter and antimatter. This flow of matter and energy is taking place in all three spaces. Matter and energy can be also considered to flow along the seven dimensions of each space. Thus total number of rivers in the Ṛgveda becomes twenty one. Here are some verses from the Ṛgveda to support my argument.

"O rivers (Sindhus), you live in three places." Ṛgveda 3.56.5

"Seven rivers are flowing in heaven." Ṛgveda 1.72.8

"We call three times seven flowing rivers." Ṛgveda 10.64.8

"Rivers flow seven by seven in three places." Ṛgveda 10.75.1

As I have earlier noted, only three dimensions of our space are experienced by us. Rest of the four dimensions are referred to as sub-directions and described as existing above. Four rivers representing these dimensions are also described as existing above in the Ṛgveda.

"Indra filled four rivers flowing above with sweet water." Ṛgveda 1.62.6

Another important point is that all seven dimensions exist at each point in space, they just point in different directions. The rivers of Ṛgveda also originate from same place, flow together, and end up in the same place. There is no evidence in Ṛgveda to show that seven rivers of the Ṛgveda are separated in space.

"When Vṛtra counterattacked, one god Indra became the hair of horse. Mighty Indra won the cows, won Soma, and freed seven rivers to flow." Ṛgveda 1.32.12

"Who killed the serpent and made seven rivers flow, who got the cows hidden by Bala out, who created Agni between two rocks, who kills enemies in wars, he, O people, is Indra." Ṛgveda 2.12.3

These verses show that all seven rivers start their journey from the same place, where serpent Vṛtra was killed. Saraswatī, Indus and other five rivers considered to be belonging to this group of seven rivers do not match this description. Consider the following prayer by sage Viśwāmitra to rivers Vipāta and Śutudri.

"Coming forth from the lap of mountains desiring (to go to sea) like two joyous horses set free. Like two white cows licking their calves Vipāta and Śutudri rivers are flowing full of water." Ṛgveda 3.33.1

"Set in motion by Indra you are flowing directly towards ocean like charioteers. Moving in accordance to other, with overflowing waves, shining, one of you meets the other." Ṛgveda 3.33.2

"I went near best of mothers Sindhu, Like two mothers licking their offsprings, they move towards same place. I have come near best of mothers Sindhu, I have come near wide lucky Vipāta." Ṛgveda 3.33.3

These verses describe the rivers as flowing together without any separation. These rivers do not carry water. These rivers represent the flow of matter particles. In the next chapter we will take up the discussion of fundamental particles as found in the Vedas.

"These people go in and out all very nicely dressed. Do you conclude from this that they swim dressed."
- Heisenberg

"I have seen an untiring milkman, who travels on converging and diverging roads near and far away. He stays inside the world dressed up."
Ṛgveda 1.164.31

9. QUARK CONFINEMENT

Modern physics tells us that matter and energy can be converted into each other, but does not tell us much about the shape of fundamental particles and whether there are any stages during the transformation of matter particle into energy. Fundamental particles are considered point particles which have zero length and volume, but possess mass, momentum and charge, thus making the mass-energy and charge density infinite for the point particles. When a property tends to infinity, physicists call it a singularity. Modern particle physics is then a mine of moving singularities. Physicists dislike singularity, because it is difficult to handle and conceptually meaningless. They have come up with smart ways to avoid singularities, but that cannot be considered a solution. This is the result of modern science reaching the limits of detection. These limits have become so obvious that a controversial book "The End of Science" has been written [1].

However, the approach of modern science is not the only way to investigate the ultimate reality. The analytical approach of modern science has limitations, and the Vedic physics goes beyond these limitations as the Vedic scientists have seen whatever can be seen in this universe. It is only appropriate that the Vedic scientists gave the name Paśu to whatever could be seen.

9.1: Particle

Paśu (animal) is derived from the root "Paś" meaning to see. That is why Puruṣa was termed Paśu when he changed his form from unobservable to observable. That Paśus are related to being observable, and nothing to do whatsoever with animals in their intended meaning, is clearly seen in the Śatapatha Brāhmaṇa.

"Prajāpati saw Agni in those Paśus, therefore they are called Paśus." Śatapatha Brāhmaṇa 6.2.1.4

This mantra also shows explicitly the equivalence of particles (Paśus) and energy (Agni). There are several mantras in the Vedic scriptures to this effect.

"Agni was Paśu." Yajurveda 23.17

"Paśus are Āgneya." Taittiriya Brāhmaṇa 1.1.4.5

Āgneya means having the quality of Agni. Earlier, the reader has seen that Maruta are related to radiation. The Vedic sages knew perfectly well that particles radiated energy.

"Paśus are Māruta." Aitareya Brāhmaṇa 3.19

"Paśus are Āgneya and Māruta." Jaimini Brāhmaṇa 2.231

Māruta means having the quality of Maruta. The transformation of matter particles into energy and energy into particles is well established by these mantras.

9.2: Bosons and Fermions

How did particles originate? Puruṣa hymn describes the origin of particles (Paśus) in the following verse.

"From that Yajña of entire offering coagulated butter (or butter mixed with curd) was obtained. Vāyavya, Āranya and Grāmya animals (Paśu) were made." Ṛgveda 10.90.8

Coagulated butter refers to the universe becoming inhomogeneous. In earlier state universe was Salila, completely homogeneous. With the rise of inhomogeneity, particles were formed. Particles can be thought of as condensation of energy. Particles were given the name Paśu because they could be seen. Primary meaning of Paśu is an animal. Animals have been classified under three categories: Grāmya, Āraṇya and Vāyavya. Grāmya animal means those animals which prefer to stay together or domestic animals. Grāma is a word in Sanskrit which means a village called so because people live together there. As opposed to Grāmya, Āraṇya means wild animal, derived from Araṇya meaning forest. Wild animals prefer to stay alone. Knowledgeable readers will come to the conclusion that Grāmya particles are what physicists call bosons and Āraṇya particles are what physicists call fermions. Vāyavya means pertaining to Vāyu. I have already identified Vāyu with field, so Vāyavya particles can be called field particles. Field particles are related to how particles interact with each other. Earlier scientists believed in the principle of action at a distance. Particles just interacted with each other without any intermediary and interaction was instantaneous. Newton was the champion of this school of thought. Later scientists hypothesized that particles interacted with an intermediary called field. Interaction is not instantaneous and highest speed of interaction is the velocity of light. Einstein was the champion of this school of thought. Scientists in last few decades have come up with the idea of field particles, and under this concept particles interact via the exchange of field particles. Electromagnetic interaction takes place by the exchange of photons. It is evident that Vedic scientists considered field to act via field particles and knew five thousand years ago what scientists are beginning to realize only now.

Grāmya particles are further divided in four types: Aja meaning goat, Avi meaning sheep, Aśva meaning horse and Gau meaning cow. This is again described in the Puruṣa hymn.

"From that horses were born, who have teeth on both sides. From that cows were born, from that goats and sheep were born." Ṛgveda 10.90.10

It is important to note here that only these four domestic animals find repeated mention in the Ṛgveda. Cat, for example, is not mentioned in the Vedas. Cows are hidden in the mountains, horses drive the chariots of gods, wool of sheep is used to strain Soma juice and goat is the vehicle of Pūṣā. All of these have a precise scientific meaning. The choice of these four animals to represent four Grāmya particles is not arbitrary, which will become evident soon. Aja means not born. Sometimes Aja is also referred to as Ekaja meaning once-born. Aja is the intermediate step during the transformation of energy into particle. I will translate Aja as localized energy. Aja is almost like energy, and that is why it was given the name not-born, however some change has taken place which could not escape the attention of the Vedic scientists. You should recall that energy is considered immortal in Vedic science, and therefore not-born. Aja then transforms into Avi, Aśva or Gau particle. As Avi, Aśva or Gau particle are born from Aja, these three particles can be considered twice-born with Aja being considered once-born. The confusion between animals and particles gave rise to a hierarchical division of Hindu society.

9.3: Once-born and twice-born

Hindu society is divided in four classes (Varṇa): Brāhmaṇa, Kṣatriya, Vaiśya and Śūdra. This division existed in the Vedic age, which is evident from the reference to these Varṇas in Puruṣa hymn. However, Varṇa system was not based on birth in the Vedic age. In post-vedic times, four Varṇas became representative of four Grāmya animals. Brāhmaṇa became representative of cow (Gau), Ksatriya became representative of horse (Aśva), Vaiśya became representative of sheep (Avi) and Śūdra became representative of goat (Aja). This representation, though not unique, is very well accepted in post-vedic literature. Śatapatha Brāhmaṇa 13.2.2.15 says that horse is Kṣatriya. It also says that cow was born from the mouth of Prajāpati (12.7.1.4), and the Puruṣa hymn says that Brāhmaṇa was born from the mouth of Puruṣa (Ṛgveda 10.90.12). Thus cow became representative of Brāhmaṇa. The Vedas ban the killing of cows. It is for this reason that killing of cow or Brāhmaṇa became the greatest sin in post-vedic Hinduism. Once these identifications gained ground, Śūdra became once-born and rest of the three Varṇas became twice-born. Second birth commenced with the rite of Upanayana and study of the Vedas was taken up only after Upanayana. As Śūdras were deprived the rite of Upanayana because now they were not twice-born, they also lost the right to study Vedas. This was one of the most unfortunate developments in the Hindu society and Hindus have paid a very heavy price for this institutionalized inequality. If a corrective step is not taken today, this inequality may finish Hinduism altogether.

9.4: The flying horse

Avi (sheep) particle is given this name, because this particle closely resembles field. Sheep are covered with wool, and similarly Avi particles are covered with dense field lines. Soma is repeatedly described as being strained through sheep's wool in the

Ṛgveda, which means the passage of Soma through field lines of Avi particle.

Aśva (horse) particle is given this name because of the fast speed of the horse. Aśva is often described in the Ṛgveda as travelling faster than thoughts. Gau (cow) particle gets its name because it emits radiation like cow gives milk. These particles could not have meant animals by any stretch of imagination. It is obvious from even a cursory reading of the Ṛgveda. I am translating here a full hymn dedicated to Aśva particle to show that Aśva does not mean horse in the Vedas.

Ṛgveda 1.163

Sage: Dirghatamā Aucathya; Deity: Aśva; Meter: Triṣṭupa

1. When you roared springing from sea or land after birth, your great birth is worthy of praise. You have wings of eagle and arms of deer.

2. This horse was given by Yama, Trita harnessed it, Indra captured him first, and Gandharva held its reins. Vasus made this horse from the sun.

3. You are Yama, you are Āditya, you are Trita by a hidden act, you are well associated with Soma. You have three bindings in heaven, it is said.

4. You have three bindings in heaven, you have three bindings in waters, you have three bindings in sea. Tell me, Varuṇa, where was your most excellent birth.

5. O horse, these are your purifying regions, these are impressions of your feet related to sacrifice. Here I have seen your auspicious reins, which protect universal law.

6. I recognise your soul in my mind from faraway coming down from heaven like a flying bird. I have seen your head going through easy to travel roads without dust like a bird.

7. I have seen your beautiful form eager to eat food in cow's foot. (here cow's foot is normally translated place of earth as earth is one of the meaning of cow in post-vedic literature). When your mortals received the enjoyment, then you greedy ate the herbs.

8. O horse, chariot follows you, men follow you, cows follow you, luck of young ladies follows you. Those following the laws follow you desiring your friendship. Gods follow you measuring your strength.

9. His horns are golden, his feet are of iron, he is faster than mind and even Indra, who first mounted him, was lower than him. Gods come to partake his oblation.

10. The horses have full-haunch and slender-waist. They are fiery and follow heavenly course. When they travel along the heavenly path, they move in rows like swans.

11. O horse, your body is made for flying, your mind is rapid as wind. Your beautiful horns are placed in various ways and travel in forests.

12. Strong horse goes for slaughtering meditating upon the gods. His navel goat is led ahead, admirers and poets follow him.

13. The horse goes directly to his father and mother in the most excellent place. Go to the gods happily today. May the donors receive wealth.

This certainly is no ordinary horse. Either the sages were drunk as modern historians tell us, or they are describing what Aśva particle is precisely. The picture certainly is of a flying horse.

Flying is referred explicitly in verses six, ten and eleven. In verse one wings are mentioned. Flying will apply exactly to a fundamental particle. In verses two and three Aśva particle is associated with Trita. Trita became King Triton in Greek mythology. Trita is referred to as a king in the Ṛgveda as well. Trita means one third, and was given this name because Trita refers to one third electric charge. I will identify Aśva as one of the quark particles. Modern scientists have very recently found that quarks carry one third electric charge only. An electron or a proton carries one unit charge. Verse three tells that Aśva is Trita by a hidden act. Vedic sages clearly know that quarks cannot be observed in isolation, that there actual form is always hidden. Calling Aśva by the name Trita means that Aśva particle carries one third charge. Verse twelve and thirteen apparently describe horse sacrifice. This is not an actual sacrifice, but the transformation of Aśva particle in energy, and that is why horse (Aśva) is supposed to go to gods (energy). In verse twelve Aja is called the navel of Aśva particle. Navel means center, and here it denotes the fact that Aśva particle is made from Aja. Goat is said to be led ahead of horse in the sacrifice. Scientifically, this signifies that before transformation into energy Aśva particle becomes Aja. Thus the process of transformation in the Vedas is from energy to Aja, and Aja to particles, and then back to Aja, and Aja to energy. This process of creation and annihilation of particles carries on continuously.

The horns of horse are referred in verses nine and eleven. Horns are golden signifying that particles can be transformed into energy. Horses don't have horns and therefore horns are translated as ear or mane, but the word used in the Ṛgveda is Śṛṅga, which means horn and not ear or mane. This description was deliberate to distinguish Aśva particle from animal horse, as a very poor fate awaited the animal. Vedas talk about the sacrifice of Grāmya animals (cow, horse, goat and sheep), and any confusion between apparent and intended meaning would bring horrible cruelty to these animals. Despite the best efforts of the Vedic scientists the horrible practice of animal sacrifice gained ground.

9.5: Animal sacrifice

Particle physics is a branch of modern physics that has fascinated both layman and experts in this century by the extraordinary discoveries. Particle physics interests all of us because it is about knowing what the universe is made of, and might someday explain what our consciousness is made of, what makes us aware. Particle physics owes its beginning to John Dalton, who in 1808 proposed the atomic theory of matter. According to his theory matter was composed of atoms. Atoms of an element combined with atoms of another element to form compounds. Towards the end of nineteenth century, J. J. Thomson discovered electron, one of the building block of atoms. The discovery of other two building blocks of atom, proton and neutron, took another thirty five years. With the discovery of neutron in 1932, a nice and perfect picture of atomic world consisting of electron, proton and neutron emerged. However, soon this picture was shattered with the discovery of a number of new sub-atomic particles. Particle physicists continued to discover new particles, and soon their number reached more than hundred. The picture started to grow complex instead of becoming simple. Were all of them fundamental particles or even these particles were made of smaller building blocks. These particles are categorized in bosons, living together, and fermions, living alone. Fermions are further divided in two groups, baryons, which are affected by strong force, and leptons, which are not affected by strong force. Similarly bosons are further divided in two groups: mesons, which are affected by strong force, and intermediate bosons, also called gauge bosons, which are not affected by strong force. Proton and neutron are baryons, electron and neutrinos are leptons, and photon is a gauge boson. Baryons and mesons, both of them affected by strong force, are collectively called hadrons. In 1964 scientists M. Gell-Mann and George Zweig proposed that hadrons were made up of three fundamental particles. These particles were given the name quarks, and later their number rose to six with the discovery of new particles. There is something very strange about quarks. They don't exist by themselves. They are always combined with other quarks. Efforts to isolate the quarks are futile, because to break quarks, they need to be bombarded with high-speed particles and the energy of these particles is transformed into making quarks. Quarks can be thought as ends of a string, if you cut the string, you make two new ends again. Grāmya Paśus can be identified with quarks. They cannot exist alone. They are always in a form different from what they actually are. In effect their actual form has been sacrificed. Modern physicists call this phenomenon "quark confinement" and Vedic scientists called this phenomenon "Paśumedha" meaning animal sacrifice. The sacrifice in Vedic science means a change of form, and has nothing to do with actual human or animal sacrifice. For this reason, in the Ṛgveda, Yajña has been called Adhwara at several places. Adhwara means without violence, and actual animal sacrifice cannot be performed without violence. As we saw earlier for the reason that humans or animals may not be sacrificed by confusion with Puruṣamedha, the Vedic scientists allowed the depiction of Puruṣa animal only as a mythical unicorn. What could they do to prohibit animal sacrifice? Indus valley civilization was spread over a large area, and animal sacrifice could take place in remote areas. Cruelty to animals was unacceptable to the Vedic scientists having reached such a high level of intelligence, and therefore they took a very extreme step. They completely banned the depiction of Grāmya animals, cow, horse, goat and sheep. This is the reason there are no figures found of these four animals in any seals of Indus valley civilization. The absence of horse depiction was noted by proponents of Aryan Invasion Theory. They tried to prove that horse was not known in Indus valley civilization and it was brought into India by invading Aryans. Now we know the actual reason for this.

We should note that only quarks are always dressed, other fundamental particles like leptons can be isolated to be observed naked. Similarly only Grāmya animals are sacrificed, Vāyavya and Āraṇya animals are not sacrificed.

9.6: Quarks

There is an interesting story about the creation of charged particles in Śatapatha Brāhmaṇa 1.2.3.1.

"Agni was earlier of four types. First one chosen for sacrifice fled. Second and third also fled. Then Agni we know hid inside water, but gods found him and took him out of water forcefully. Agni spat on waters saying you could not provide me protection. From that three Āptya gods came out – Ekata, Dvita and Trita. They started living with Indra."

First three Agnis represent the 75 % of mass-energy in light space. Fourth Agni is the 25 % of mass-energy in observer space. Hiding of Agni in water represents the equivalence of matter and energy. Second part describes the formation of charged particles. Ekata means one, Dvita means two third and Trita means one third. These refer to particles carrying unit, two third and one third charge. Their description Āptya means electrically charged. Finally staying with Indra means these particles give rise to electrical force as they are electrically charged.

Quarks are six, and each quark has three variations making the total eighteen. These variations are given the name color by scientists, and quarks are said to have three colors. It is amazing that Vedic scientists also came up with the same idea of color to distinguish Grāmya particles.

"Indra creates white milk in black and red cows." Ṛgveda 1.62.9

"Two horses, black, red or white, draw the chariot of Agni." Ṛgveda 2.10.2

In Śwetāśwatara Upaniṣad 304.5 Aja is said to be of three colors red, white and black creating various objects of its own form. In Maitrāyaṇī Saṃhitā 4.5.7 Avi is said to be of three colors red, white and black. However, there are important differences between quarks and Grāmya particles. Quarks are six and Grāmya particles are only four. Also, all quarks are considered fundamental, while three Grāmya particles Gau, Aśva and Avi are said to be derived from Aja particle. This means that further simplification in the quark model will arise as scientists dig deeper into the properties of quarks. The Śatapatha Brāhmaṇa clearly states that other particles are formed from Aja particle.

"Aja is the form of all animals." Śatapatha Brāhmaṇa 6.5.1.4

Aja being the intermediate step of transformation of energy into particles and particles into energy, this mantra makes perfect sense. Following mantras from the Vedas support this viewpoint.

"Aja is Agni." Atharvaveda 9.5.7

"Aja was born from perturbation (Śoka) of Agni." Atharvaveda 9.5.13

"Aja was born from perturbation (Śoka) of Agni and he saw Agni first and gods became gods due to Aja." Yajurveda 13.51, Atharvaveda 4.14.1

These mantras very well illustrate that Aja is more like energy than particle. Aja has been described as having only one foot (ekapāda) in scriptures (Ṛgveda 7.35.13, Śatapatha Brāhmaṇa 8.2.4.1). I have never encountered a goat having only one foot. This again is further proof of Aja being an intermediate step during the transformation of energy into particle. Once the particle form has completely manifested, then this manifestation is referred to as an animal having four feet. In Yajurveda following question is raised.

"What object is Pilippilā and what object is Piśaṅgilā?" Yajurveda 23.11

Pilippilā is something that is very soft and presses very easily. Piśaṅgilā means devourer. The answer is given in the next mantra.

"Avi is Pilippilā and night is Piśaṅgilā." Yajurveda 23.12

However the inquirer is still curious and asks the question again to get a definite answer. Then he gets following answer.

"Aja is Piśaṅgilā, who like a dog gets things out and devours it again." Yajurveda 23.56

Here we find that Vedic scientists could not only observe the Grāmya particles, but measure their properties as well. Avi particle is considered a soft particle because it has dense field-lines coming out of it. Total number of fundamental particles is considered eight in Jaimini Brāhmaṇa.

"There are eight Paśus." Jaiminī Brāhmaṇa 3.318

Obviously the sages could not be talking about animals, as they could easily count more than eight kinds of animals around them. Eight animals refer to eight-fold division of fundamental particles known to particle physicists.

9.7: The sacred cow

The Ṛgveda is the celebration of the manifestation of the universe. It describes the evolution of the cosmos as it has happened. The sages want the universe to form, because without universe you and I cannot be there. They are happy when the forces of expansion win the war over the forces of contraction, because without the expansion of universe, there will be no universe. One of the fundamental particles that plays a very critical role in the expansion of the universe is Gau particle, and it is no wonder that cow became a sacred animal in Hinduism.

There are two complete hymns dedicated to Gau in Ṛgveda (10.169 and 6.28). Two verses in hymn 6.28 are dedicated to Gau as well as Indra. Ṛgveda 10.19 is dedicated to Gau or Āpaḥ, and Ṛgveda 4.58 to Gau or Agni or Sūrya or Ghṛta.

To a non-Hindu it is very difficult to understand why cow is considered sacred by the Hindus. The Hindus do not eat beef, because they consider cow as mother, who nourishes us by her milk. This is the traditional justification. As most Hindu beliefs, the origin of this belief can also be traced back to the Vedas. The Vedas clearly have very high respect for cow. One of the adjectives for cow in the Vedas is aghnyā meaning not to be killed. One verse from the Ṛgveda says:

"Cow is the mother of Rudras, daughter of Vasus, sister of Ādityas, and should not be killed." Ṛgveda 8.101.15

Cow should not be killed is repeated several times in the Vedas. This is again a paradox, because the Vedas also talk of cow-sacrifice along with horse, goat and sheep sacrifice. The way out of paradox is simple now. The sacrifice refers to Grāmya particles not existing in their actual forms. As the chances of confusion of these particles with animals were extremely great, sages specifically referred to cow as aghanyā. Sages took extreme precaution in dealing with the concept of Puruṣa and Grāmya animals, as any wrong interpretation could have resulted in human or animal sacrifice. There are several verses in the Ṛgveda, where Gau cannot be confused with cow animal. In post-vedic period as the real meaning of Gau was forgotten, additional meanings of word Gau were invented to make sense of the Vedic verses. Where Gau of sun is mentioned (Ṛgveda 7.36.1), Gau is interpreted to mean sun's rays. Where Gau is said to be mixed with Soma (Ṛgveda 9.10.3), Gau is interpreted as cow's milk. In all such descriptions, Gau means Gau particle, and its scientific meaning can be understood without taking recourse to secondary meanings of word Gau. Cows having one, two, four, eight or nine legs are mentioned in Ṛgveda 1.164.41. Cow has been called aṣṭakarṇī, having eight ears, in Ṛgveda 10.62.7. These verses are not describing ordinary cow animal, but they are describing Gau particle. Scientific meaning of these verses will become clear, when science reaches the capability of observing Gau particle in greater detail. Kauśītakī Brāhmaṇa 12.1 and Śatapatha Brāhmaṇa 12.4.4.4 say that "Āpo vai dhenavaḥ" meaning waters are indeed cows. Why would anyone write something like this? This is not the result of drinking too much Soma, rather it has a precise meaning. This is neither about water nor about cows, which are just symbols. Scientific meaning is that Gau particles are one form of matter particles.

In Vedic cosmology Gau particle has a very special place. Initially the universe is a complete void without space, matter and energy. The expansion of the universe is not a smooth affair to begin with as forces of expansion and contraction are delicately balanced. As the universe starts to expand, the creation of matter and energy begins. This creation takes place at the surface of the universe. There is an energy barrier for this process to take place, and therefore the surface of the universe is given the name mountain by the Vedic sages. Gau particles, along with other particles, are produced at the surface of the universe. For this reason cows are said to be hiding in the mountains in the Ṛgveda. According to Ṛgveda 10.67.4-5, Bṛhaspati opened three doors and freed cows. These three doors are the endpoints of observer, intermediate and light spaces. As Gau particles are charged particles, remember that they have been identified with quarks having fractional charge, they produce electric force, Indra, and contribute to the expansion of universe. For this reason Indra is called to be protector of cows. Once the process has stabilized, expansion of universe continues along with the creation of matter and energy. In the Vedas, the sages are always asking for cows, horses and wealth. They are not asking for personal wealth, but they are asking for space, matter and energy in a universe without it, so that one day we human beings could exist. It is because of the role played by Gau particle in our existence that Cow is considered sacred. In ancient India wealth of a person was measured by the number of cows possessed by that person. This happened because cow is described as wealth repeatedly in the Ṛgveda (1.33.1, 6.44.12, 5.79.7, 7.92.3, 5.52.17, 7.94.9, 7.67.9, 5.57.7, 7.77.5). Atharvaveda 18.1.32 says that cow holds the earth. This verse describes the role of Gau particle in keeping observer space separated from light space. In Purāṇas, earth sometimes takes the shape of a cow, which is a representation of verses like this from Vedas. Ṛgveda 10.46.3 says that Trita found Agni on the head of cow: This verse says that Gau particle possesses one third fractional charge and that particle can be transformed into energy. Transformation of matter into energy and energy into matter is well accepted in Vedas, and this transformation is the subject of discussion in the next chapter.

"All particles of matter and energy are but different harmonies of strings."
- Sylvester James Gates

10. MATTER AND ENERGY

The Vedic physics and modern physics both tell us that there is a continuous dance of creation and annihilation of particles everywhere in the universe. Matter particles transform into energy and energy transforms into particles. The Vedas describe this dance as follows. Energy changes into Aja, Aja into matter particles, particles into Aja, and Aja back into energy. This creation-annihilation energy has a very special place in the cosmology of the Ṛgveda, and the Vedic sages gave it the name of God Savitā.

10.1: Savitā

Savitā is derived from root "sū" meaning to procreate. Word "Prasava" from the same root means to give birth. As energy gives birth to matter particles, name Savitā could not be more appropriate. Nirukta 10.31 says that Savitā gives birth to all.

There are ten complete hymns dedicated to Savitā (Ṛgveda 1.35, 2.38, 4.53, 4.54, 5.81, 5.82, 6.71, 7.38, 7.45, and 10.149). There are twelve more mantras dedicated to Savitā in other hymns (Ṛgveda 1.22.5-8, 1.24.3-4, 3.62.10-12, and 10.139.1-3), and there are few more mantras in which he has been invoked together with other gods (Ṛgveda 1.24.5, 1.35.1, 7.38.6, 9.67.25, and 9.67.26). God Savitā is very special to Vedic sages. They describe him in the most beautiful words. The most sacred mantra of the Ṛgveda, the Gāyatrī mantra, is dedicated to God Savitā.

"Tatsaviturvareṇyam bhargo devasya dhīmahi, dhiyo yo naḥ prachodayāt." Ṛgveda 3.62.10

meaning,

"Let's meditate on that brilliant radiance of God Savitā. May he provide inspiration to our intellect."

To provide inspiration is the distinctive feature of Savitā. Here is a beautiful hymn dedicated to God Savitā.

Ṛgveda 1.35

Sage: Hiraṇyastūpa Āṅgirasa; Deity: Savitā;

Meter: 1, 9: Jagatī, Rest: Triṣṭupa

1. I invoke Agni first for well-being, I invoke Mitra and Varuṇa for help, I invoke night (Rātri) giving rest to the world, I invoke god Savitā for help.
2. Moving in dark atmosphere, placing immortals and mortals in their respective places, god Savitā comes on a golden chariot observing the universe.
3. He goes by high-lying or low-lying ways, adorable travels by two bright horses. God Savitā comes from faraway driving away all evil.
4. Covered with gold, having many shapes, bearing dark atmosphere, adorable Savitā having beautiful brightness is riding on the chariot with golden axle.

5. His horses, which are dark in color but have white legs, carrying the chariot with golden front have seen the people well. Whole world and all people are always situated near god Savitā.

6. There are three heavens, two of them are near Savitā, in one Yama has his beautiful palace. As the chariot rests on the pin of the axle, immortals on Savitā, one who knows this, come and tell us here.

7. The bird with beautiful wings has seen the atmospheres well. He is life-giver, gives good guidance and deeply excited. Where is sun now, who knows? In which heaven its rays have spread?

8. He has seen the eight summits of earth, three joint regions and seven seas. God Savitā having golden eyes has come giving precious gems to worshipper.

9. Savitā having golden hands travels between both earth and heaven observing all. He removes diseases, instigates sun and pervades in heaven from dark atmosphere.

10. Having golden hands, life-giver, giving good guidance, giving pleasure, self-supported Savitā come here. Praised Savitā takes his place every night driving away demons and evil spirits.

11. O Savitā, the dustless roads, you had earlier, well-made in atmosphere, today protect us by those easy to travel roads, speak in our favor.

God Savitā has golden chariot (verse 2), his chariot has golden axle (verse 4) and his chariot has golden front (verse 5). Savitā has golden hands (verse 10) and golden eyes (verse 8). Savitā also has golden tongue (Ṛgveda 6.71.3). Thus Savitā and gold are very intimately connected. As gold is the color of energy in Vedic science, there is an exact match between the description of God Savitā and his identification with creation-annihilation energy. Scientists are well aware of the laws governing transformation of energy. Vedic sages are also well aware of these laws, when they say the following about the laws of Savitā.

"Whose laws cannot be violated by Indra, Varuṇa, Mitra, Aryamā and Rudra, whose laws cannot be broken by any enemy, I invoke that God Savitā by praises for good fortune." Ṛgveda 2.38.9

In post-vedic times Savitā became identical with Sūrya (sun). However, in the Ṛgveda, Savitā and Sūrya are as distinct as they can be. Sūrya is not described as golden like Savitā. Sūrya is time and again mentioned as residing in heaven, whereas Savitā resides in the atmosphere. In Ṛgveda 1.35.9 Savitā is said to instigate Sūrya. Savitā is said to join with rays of Sūrya in Ṛgveda 5.81.4. In Ṛgveda 1.123.3 Savitā and Sūrya both are mentioned. Thus Savitā is very distinct from Sūrya, and this distinction will become very clear when identification of Sūrya is taken up in a later chapter. For now, we will devote some time discussing another prominent Vedic God closely related with Savitā, but forgotten in a later age, namely Pūṣā.

10.2: Pūṣā

There are eight complete hymns dedicated to Pūṣā in Ṛgveda (1.42, 1.138, 6.53, 6.54, 6.55, 6.56, 6.58, and 10.26). There are fourteen other mantras dedicated to Pūṣā (Ṛgveda 1.23.13-15, 3.62.7-9, 6.48.16-19, and 10.17.3-6). In two hymns and four mantras Pūṣā has been invoked with other gods (Ṛgveda 2.40, 6.57 and 8.4.15-18). Pūṣā means one who nourishes and is derived from root "Puṣ" meaning to nourish. Pūṣā is intimately connected with animals as seen from following mantra:

"Animals are Pūṣā, nourishment is Pūṣā, nourishment is animal." Śatapatha Brāhmaṇa 3.1.4.9

Pūṣā is called guardian of animals (Paśupā) in Ṛgveda 6.58.2. Taittiriya Saṃhitā 1.5.1 says that Pūṣā is the master of animals. As animals are particles, Pūṣā can be identified as "set of particles". All the particles are collectively termed Pūṣā. There are eight hymns dedicated to Pūṣā, because of the eightfold division of fundamental particles. The eightfold way of classifying fundamental particles was proposed by Murray Gell-Mann and Yuval Ne'eman in 1961 [1]. The name "eightfold way" was suggested by association with the eightfold way of Buddhism. In Ṛgveda 6.58.1 Pūṣā is said to have two forms, one black and other white. White form is that of particle and black form is that of anti-particle. Here is a beautiful hymn dedicated to Pūṣā.

Ṛgveda 6.54

Sage: Bārhaspatya Bhardwāja; Deity Pūṣā, Meter: Gāyatrī

1. Pūṣā, take us to the wise person, who shows us straight path, who tells emphatically that this is (our lost wealth).
2. Let's join with Pūṣā, who shows the way to our homes, who says that this is.
3. The wheel of Pūṣā never gets damaged, seat on his chariot never falls, felly of his wheel never wavers.
4. Pūṣā never forgets him, who pays oblation to Pūṣā. He receives wealth first.
5. Let Pūṣā walk behind our cows, let Pūṣā protect our horses, let Pūṣā give us grains.
6. Pūṣā, walk behind the cows of us admirers and sacrifice performers, who are extracting juice of Soma.
7. Let none of them get lost, let none of them get hurt, let none of them fall in pits. Come to us with unhurt cows.

8. We ask for wealth from Lord Pūṣā, who hears our praises, who is careful and whose wealth is never lost.
9. Pūṣā, let's abide by your laws, and never get hurt. We sing your praises.
10. Let Pūṣā hold his right hand very far away, and bring back our lost animals.

In verse three wheel of Pūṣā is mentioned, which represents the spin of the particles. Pūṣā is the master of great riches in Ṛgveda 6.55.2. This makes perfect sense as particles are the wealth of the universe. The relationship of Pūṣā with Savitā is described by the following verses in the Vedas:

"Savitā instigates Pūṣā for movement." Ṛgveda 10.139.1

"Pūṣā moves by inspiration of Savitā." Yajurveda 17.58

"Savitā becomes Pūṣā by his movement." Ṛgveda 5.81.5

These verses establish that when energy (Savitā) transforms into particles, it is called Pūṣā. Pūṣā is called Ajāśva in Ṛgveda 1.138.4, 6.55.3 and 6.58.2. Ajāśva is made by joining of words Aja meaning goat and Aśva meaning horse. Ajāśwa means one whose goats do the work of horses. Following verses do not leave any doubt about the work goats do for Pūṣā.

"The chariot of Pūṣā is drawn by Aja." Ṛgveda 6.55.6, 6.57.3, 10.26.8

The reader should recall that Aja has been earlier described as the intermediate stage during the transformation of energy into matter particles. For this reason Aja is said to drive the chariot of Pūṣā. The process of creation and annihilation of particles can now be described as following:

Savitā → Aja → Pūṣā → Aja → Savitā

In Brāhmaṇas, like many other gods Pūṣā also became one of the names of sun. However, description of Pūṣā in Ṛgveda cannot be that of sun by any stretch of imagination. In Ṛgveda 6.56.3 Pūṣā is described as rotating the golden wheel of sun. In Ṛgveda 6.58.3 Pūṣā is said to be the messenger of sun. Importance of Pūṣā gradually decreased after the Vedic age and in the Purāṇas he hardly gets any mention. His main job as the keeper of animals was assigned to Śiva, and as Śiva is currently worshipped by Hindus all over the world, historians were quick to identify the seal of Pūṣā as that of Śiva, Lord of the animals.

10.3: Lord of the animals

Figure 10.1 shows Pūṣā, Lord of the animals. This figure is widely recognized as that of representing an earlier form of Śiva, and has been given the name Proto-Śiva. This identification is completely wrong. The figure has no resemblance to that of Śiva. There is no Triśūla, the weapon of Śiva, there is no Nandī Bull, who accompanies Śiva, there is no moon on the forehead, there is no Gaṅgā river flowing from his lock of hair. Only reason this figure has been identified with Śiva, is that Śiva is called Lord of the animals, and there are several animal figures surrounding the central figure. However, this cannot be considered a clinching evidence, because there is a god in the Ṛgveda, Pūṣā, who is explicitly referred to as Lord of the animals. Śiva is not even mentioned in Ṛgveda, because Śiva is a later concept that has formed by amalgamation of the Ṛgvedic gods Pūṣā and Rūdra. My contention is that from the Ṛgveda to the Brāhmaṇas to the Purāṇas we have a complete description of the evolution of Hinduism and the history of India, and there is absolutely no need to take recourse to vague prefixes like "Proto".

Figure 10.1: Pūṣā, Lord of the animals,

a seal from Mohenjo-daro (M-304)

Our ancestors believed in learning, they have kept records assiduously, and they have left us enough material to construct our history right from Indus Valley Civilization to the present day. All we need to do is to use logical reasoning without bias, be objective, and separate science from mythology and mythology from history. Proto-Śiva, Proto-Sanskrit, Proto-Indo-European language, all these are purely speculative concepts. Sanskrit is the mother of all languages in the Indo-European family, and there was never any language called Proto-Sanskrit.

We have already seen that there was a complete ban on the depiction of horse, cow, sheep and goat, and therefore these animals are not shown in the figure. There is an animal figure below the central figure, which looks like a deer. In Ṛgveda goat is repeatedly said to be the vehicle of Pūṣā, and if depiction of goat was banned, deer could be considered a natural replacement. Central figure wears a headgear in the seal, and Pūṣā is described as wearing headgear in Ṛgveda 6.55.2. As the Ṛgveda forms the basis of understanding the Indus Valley Civilization, it is only logical to identify the central figure with that of Pūṣā.

Savitā and Pūṣā represent energy and matter particles in the Ṛgveda. You might be wondering what are the Vedic counterparts of electron, proton and neutron, the building blocks of atoms. Is there a similar triad in Vedas? It is time to find out.

"If Christianity was somehow stopped at its birth, whole world would be following Mithraism today."
- Ernest Renan

11. ELECTRON, PROTON AND NEUTRON

History of India as known today has been written by foreigners. Native history of India is completely opposite to the history of India compiled by foreigners. Foreigners were not interested in writing an objective history of India, because they were serving their ideological masters. Foreigners were not satisfied by merely dividing Indians using pseudo-history, but they divided our gods also on racial lines. Hindus have never discriminated against people based on their color. Hindus worship God Kṛṣṇa and Goddess Kālī. Both, Kṛṣṇa and Kālī, mean black and are depicted as such as well. Foreigners have created a mess by dividing Gods along Aryan and Dravidian lines. All this is pure rubbish, as India was never invaded by Aryans. One of the gods in Vedic pantheon supposed to have been borrowed from Dravidians in Indus Valley is god Varuṇa.

11.1: Varuṇa

Varuṇa is made from root "Vṛ" and means one who covers. Nirukta 10.4 says that Varuṇa is called so because he covers.

Gopatha Brāhmaṇa 1.7 also provides similar derivation. We have already met two other words with same etymological meaning, Vṛtra and Varāha. Vṛtra and Varāha cover the universe, what could Varuṇa possibly cover? To find an answer, we have to delve deep in the Vedic concept of Varuṇa. Let's start by going through a beautiful hymn dedicated to Varuṇa in the Ṛgveda.

Ṛgveda 5.85

Sage: Bhaumātri; Deity: Varuṇa; Metre: Triṣṭupa

1. Praise supreme ruler Varuṇa by great, deep and endearing prayer. He expanded earth for sun like a hunter kills for skin.
2. Varuṇa expanded atmosphere in forests. He strengthened the horses, put milk in cows, gave desire to work in hearts, established Agni in waters and sun in heaven. He created Soma on mountains.
3. Varuṇa turned the mouth of big barrel of water downwards for earth, atmosphere and heaven and freed it. From that, the king of whole universe makes the soil fertile like rains nourish the grains.
4. Varuṇa waters earth and heaven when he wants to create the rain of milk. Mountains are covered by clouds and strong warriors slacken them.
5. I praise this great feat of famous supreme spirit Varuṇa. He measured earth by sun using a standard staying in atmosphere.
6. Nobody could destroy this great achievement of the knowledgeable god. Due to this flowing rivers cannot fill even one ocean by their waters.
7. O Varuṇa, if we have sinned towards Aryamā, Mitra or Varuṇa, friends or those always behaving like brothers, those always near or afar, free us from that.

8. If we have lied like gamblers or we have actually committed sin without knowing it, O Varuṇa, free us from sins like loosening the bond, so that we can be dear to you.

Verses three and four associate Varuṇa with waters. Ṛgveda 7.49.3-4 and Yajurveda 19.94 say that Varuṇa is the king of waters. We have already seen that the water of the Vedas is matter and anti-matter. Most matter and anti-matter particles are electrically charged. Among the electrically charged particles electron is the most important particle. The position of electron among fundamental particles is worthy of calling electron the king of particles. Thus Varuṇa can be identified with electron. Now, we should keep in mind that sages chose every word very carefully to declare its own meaning. Varuṇa means one who covers and does that apply to an electron? In fact, it does. Electron covers an atom, so that scientists refer to it as electron cloud. Now we should see how this identification fits in the framework of the Vedas.

In verse eight sages ask Varuṇa to loosen the bond and free them from sins. The net of Varuṇa is mentioned several times in the Ṛgveda (1.24.13, 1.24.15, 1.25.21, 7.88.7). In Ṛgveda 6.74.4 sage asks to be freed from the net of Varuṇa. What is this net made of?

"Varuṇa's net is not made of ropes, but people are caught by it." Ṛgveda 7.84.2

Varuṇa captures sinners in his net and punishes them. This power of Vauṇa is also referred as Māyā of Varuṇa in Ṛgveda (5.85.6, 8.41.3, 8.41.8). This net of Varuṇa is the electric field surrounding an electron and Māyā of Varuṇa is the attractive electric force. Varuṇa is also famous for the spies he employs for overseeing everyone in the universe.

"Nobody can deceive the spies of Varuṇa." Ṛgveda 6.67.5

"Varuṇa's spies see everything by their thousand eyes." Atharvaveda 4.16.4

Who are the spies of Varuṇa? Modern scientists have found out who they are. Modern scientists treat electron as an octopus, which continuously sends its probing arms at an unimaginable rate to feel out its neighbourhood [1]. These spies are the virtual particles through which electron knows what is in its neighborhood. Thus the identification of Varuṇa with electron fits very well in the framework of Vedas. Further support comes from the following description of Varuṇa.

"Mitra is day and Varuṇa is night." Taittirīya Saṃhitā 2.1.7

This description shows Mitra and Varuṇa to have opposite nature. Varuṇa is called night, and by this his dark or black color is stressed. In Vedas black is the color of negative electric charge, and electron carries negative electric charge. Also, Śatapatha Brāhmaṇa 5.2.5.17 says that everything that is black belongs to Varuṇa. Varuṇa is described as firm on following the laws in Ṛgveda 1.25.8. Electron is also very finicky about maintaining the laws. It is because of maintaining orderly universe that Varuṇa was elevated to the position of supreme deity by Iranians.

11.2: Ahuramazdā

Ahuramazdā is the supreme deity in Avestā. Ahura is same as Asura of Sanskrit as Iranians invariably pronounced Sanskrit "s" as "h". In later Indian scriptures Asuras formed the forces of evil and Devas the forces of good. However, in the Ṛgveda Asura is not used in a derogatory sense. In the Ṛgveda Varuṇa is often called by the adjective Asura (1.24.14, 2.28.7, 8.42.1). The character of Varuṇa and Ahuramazdā is strikingly similar. Moreover, in Ṛgveda Mitra and Varuṇa are worshipped as a pair "Mitrāvaruṇau" and in Avestā, Mitra and Ahura are worshipped as a pair

"Mithrāhurā", and again the character of these two pairs are strikingly similar. Therefore it can be safely said that Ahuramazdā of ancient Iranians is none other than Varuṇa. When Iranians forgot the real meaning of the Vedas, they needed to reorganize their religion. As a civilized people trying to maintain an orderly society, they raised Varuṇa to the pedestal of supreme deity, as Varuṇa stood for self-righteousness and order. Devas associated with the warlike qualities were made into the forces of evil.

The Avesta describes Ahura in the following way. Ahura is the ruler of entire world (Yasna 31.1). Ahura is the best and most powerful king, whose orders cannot be violated by anyone (Yasna 27.1 and 31.2). Ahura has fixed the place of sun, moon, earth, seas and rivers. He has fixed and controls the path of sun and stars (Yasna 37.1 and 44.1). He has created day and night (Yasna 44.5). He is awake day and night and sees the good and bad deeds of people (Yasna 31.13 and Vendidad 19.20). Nobody can deceive him, he is wise and great (Yasna 43.6 and 45.4). Mazdā means wise. Similarly description of Varuṇa is found in the Ṛgveda. Varuṇa is wise (Ṛgveda 1.124.14). Varuṇa is called king in Ṛgveda 1.24.7. Varuṇa has widened the path of the sun (Ṛgveda 1.24.8). He has divided day and night and seasons (7.66.11). Varuṇa is the source of Ṛta (Ṛgveda 2.28.5) and so is Ahura source of Āśa (Yasna 10.4). Thus the equivalence of Varuṇa and Ahuramazdā is proven beyond doubt. Now let's try to find out the identity of the famous companion of Varuṇa, that is Mitra.

11.3: Mitra

There is only one hymn dedicated to Mitra in the Ṛgveda. In twenty four other hymns Mitra is worshipped together with Varuṇa. As Varuṇa has been identified as electron, it immediately follows that Mitra be identified as proton. Mitra means friend, and protons do sit together like friends inside the nucleus of an atom.

Depiction of Mitra as day in Aitareya Brāhmaṇa 4.2.4 and Taittirīya Saṃhitā 2.1.7 also supports this identification. Day stands for brightness and white color, which was chosen by Vedic sages to represent positive electric charge. Proton carries unit positive charge, and it is for this reason that there is only one hymn dedicated to Mitra.

Ṛgveda 3.59

Sage: Gāthina Viśwāmitra; Deity: Mitra; Metre: Triṣṭupa, 6-9 - Gāyatrī

1. Mitra orders people to do their work. Mitra upholds earth and heaven. Mitra oversees the people without winking. Make the oblation containing butter for Mitra.
2. O Mitra, son of Aditi, that mortal becomes happy, who follows your laws. (He) is neither killed nor won, who is protected by you. Sin does not enter him either from near or from afar.
3. Without disease, happy, walking among the best place of earth, firm-kneed, following Āditya's laws, we want to stay under the great intellect of Mitra.
4. This venerable, serveable, intelligent king Mitra has been born. We want to live according to the auspicious intellect of that adorable (Mitra).
5. One should bow to go near great Āditya. Instigating men to do their work, (Mitra) provides happiness. For that venerable Mitra offer this oblation in Agni.
6. Favor of God Mitra, bearer of cultivators is laden with spoils. His splendor has most wonderful fame.
7. This famous Mitra pervades heaven by his greatness and earth by sounds.

8. Five men offer oblation for Mitra, one who renders powerful assistance. He holds all the gods.

9. Mitra fulfills the desires of those following the laws among the gods and mortals for people who gather and spread the sacrificial grass.

Mitra became Mithra in Iran and later Mihira meaning sun. Vedic god Mitra was once worshipped as Mithra all over Europe.

11.4: Rise and fall of Mithraism

In first century C.E. Mithraism started to gain popularity in the Roman empire. It spread with extreme rapidity and by third century C.E. it had reached the height of popularity. The greatest number of Mithraea is found in Germany. Mithraea have been found all over Europe including Italy, Switzerland, Britain, France and Spain. For more than three centuries Mithraism was practiced all over Roman empire.

Scholars have tried to explain the symbolism behind Mithraism without taking the Ṛgveda into account. Many scholars hold the view that concept of Mitra was borrowed by Indians from Iran, because Mitra is not a prominent god in the Ṛgveda. He has been dedicated only one hymn. This kind of reasoning cannot apply to the Ṛgveda. The Ṛgveda has only one hymn dedicated to Puruṣa, but there is no doubt that the Puruṣa hymn is the most important hymn of Ṛgveda. There is only one hymn for Mitra, because proton has a unit positive charge. Also, there are twenty four complete hymns in which Mitra is invoked together with Varuṇa, so Mitra is not a neglected god in Ṛgveda. It was Iranians who borrowed the concept of Mitra from India. The Ṛgveda is a complete book of cosmology, and therefore parts of it cannot be borrowed from elsewhere. Others borrowed the Ṛgvedic ideas without even knowing what they stood for. The Vedic ideas were spread in Iran after Mahābhārata war when the Indus Valley Civilization declined.

Let's try to understand Mithraic symbolism in the light of the Vedic wisdom. Mithraea, temples of Mithra, were designed to look like caves, which symbolized the universe. A cave is surrounded by stones and the Ṛgveda depicts the universe to be surrounded by mountains as we have seen earlier. Gods did not exist before the creation of the universe according to the Ṛgveda. Thus gods came into existence by breaking up the mountain covering the universe. This is the secret of the rock birth of Mithra. David Ulansey illustrates the birth of Mithra in his book "The origins of the Mithraic Mysteries" [2]. Mithra was depicted as coming out of an egg shaped rock which is entwined by a serpent. Universe was considered egg shaped by Vedic sages, and this idea was spread all over the globe. Earlier I described Vṛtra the serpent as the cover of the universe based on logical reasoning and scriptural support. Now we have found a rock solid proof of my reasoning that Vṛtra covered the whole universe. Proponents of the Aryan Invasion Theory have accused Indra of breaking the dams of Dravidian people by identifying Vṛtra the serpent as a dam holding water. Here is a positive proof that they are clueless about the meaning of the Vedas. The most prominent feature of the Mithraic iconography is the slaying of bull by Mithra. When Mithra slays the Bull, instead of blood all kinds of herbs and plants sprang from the victim. This reminds us of the sacrifice of Puruṣa by gods. Birth of Mithra from rock is similar to the birth of Vedic god Indra. Indra later became a sun god and subordinate to supreme god Viṣṇu. Mithra was also a sun god whose birthday was celebrated on 25th December.

In Mithraic theology, Mithra was not the supreme god, but subordinate to Leontocephalous Kronos, the lion headed time god. The illustrations of Leontocephalous Kronos can be seen in David

Ulansey's book "The origins of the Mithraic Mysteries" [3]. The lion-headed god is shown as having a pair of wings and his body is entwined six times by a serpent. The head of the serpent rests on the skull of the god. So far researchers have not given any thought to the Indian origin of Mithraism, rather all attempts have been made to find its origin in Iran. India was the land from which copious myths spread in all directions, and it is highly probable that Mithraism was developed by a group of Indians who had access to the secret science of Vedas, now largely forgotten.

Lion headed god of Mithraism seems to be a modified form of Nṛsiṃha incarnation of Lord Viṣṇu. Viṣṇu incarnates as a lion headed god to kill demon Hiraṇyakaśipu. He rests on the coils of serpent Śeṣanāga who provides shade to him by spreading his head above. Vehicle of Lord Viṣṇu is eagle Garuḍa. In Mithraism serpent Śeṣanāga envelops lion headed god and wings of Garuda become transplanted on the god himself. Moreover, the Śatapatha Brāhmaṇa says that "Kālo vai Viṣṇu" meaning Viṣṇu is time indeed. Thus it stands to reason that the lion headed god of Mithraism is only a modified form of Lord Viṣṇu in his Nṛsiṃha incarnation. The spread of Mithraism was the result of the third wave of emigration of ideas from India. First wave spread the knowledge of the Vedas in Iran, second wave spread the knowledge of the Brāhmaṇas in Greece and the third wave spread the knowledge of the Purāṇas in the Roman empire.

The decline of Mithraism started with the rise of Christianity. During their struggle for supremacy, Christianity absorbed many elements of Mithraism. Arnold Toynbee has called Mithraism the "Crucible of Christianity". Franz Cumont in his classic work "The Mysteries of Mithra" draws our attention to the similarities between Mithraism and Christianity [4]. Both performed baptism for purification. Both considered Sunday sacred. Both celebrated 25th of December, Mithras as birthday of Mithra and Christians as birthday of Christ. Both believed in Heaven and Hell and a flood at the beginning. Both believed in a last judgment and resurrection of the dead.

Some of the elements that Christianity borrowed from Mithraism are considered blasphemous by orthodox Christians. Once Christianity became strong enough, it exterminated Mithraism by force. Patriarch George provoked a bloody riot in December 361 CE, when he attempted to erect a church on the ruins of a Mithraeum. Many Mithras were falsely implicated in a conspiracy and put to death in 371 CE. Mithraea were sacked and burned with the complicity of the authorities. Cumont describes the persecution of Mithras saying Christianity demanded the total destruction of idolatry, and its exhortations were promptly carried into effect [5]:

By the end of fourth century C.E. Mithraism was finished by Christianity. Its fall was as swift as its rise. But Mithraism did not die after all. It lied dormant somewhere in the collective memory of the Europeans. In eighteenth century these ideas took a concrete shape and Mithraism got a new birth in the form of Freemasonry.

11.5: Aryamā

There is no separate hymn for Aryamā in the Ṛgveda, and his name is often invoked together with Mitra and Varuṇa. After identifying Mitra with proton and Varuṇa with electron, it is natural to identify Aryamā with neutron. In the Vedas Varuṇa, Mitra and Aryamā form a triad similar to that of electron, proton and neutron. They are often invoked together. Now we can understand why there is no hymn addressed to Aryamā. When sages say that their praises are reaching the deities, what is meant is the propagation of field. Neutron being charge neutral does not get affected by electric field, so there is no hymn devoted to him. Aryamā means friend, and neutrons also sit together like friends inside the atomic nucleus. In Iran Aryamā became Airyaman and kept same meaning. He was invoked during marriage ceremony in India and Iran. Here is a hymn in which Aryamā is invoked together with Mitra and Varuṇa.

Ṛgveda 1.41

Sage: Kaṇva Ghaura; Deity: Varuṇa, Mitra and Aryamā, 4-6 – Ādityas; Metre: Gāyatrī

1. Who is protected by wise Varuṇa, Mitra and Aryamā, that person cannot be suppressed.
2. Who is nourished by them, that mortal is protected from harm. He is safe from all sides.
3. These kings destroy the towns and citadels of hostile people. They take us beyond sins.
4. O Ādityas! The roads of truth are easy to travel and without thorns. There is no destroyer here.
5. O leader Ādityas! The Yajña that you perform on roads of truth, how can that be destroyed by your meditation?
6. That mortal obtains gems, all wealth and children as well easily without being harmed.
7. O friends, how are we going to write the hymns worthy of describing the greatness of Mitra, Aryamā and Varuṇa.
8. Who kills those aspiring to be gods or who curses them, let him not talk to me. Let us satisfy you by devotion.
9. Who holds the four objects, let people fear from his opponents. Let us not desire to talk in dirty language.

By now it will be clear that the Ṛgveda is a book of physics. There are many concepts in the Vedas, which we can identify by their equivalents in modern physics. It is also to be noted that the

Ṛgveda and modern physics differ on many vital points, and therefore many Vedic terms have no equivalents in modern physics, for example Vṛtra, Antarikṣa and Dyau. It is up to the physicists to probe deeper in the nature of reality and find out whether Vedas are wrong or modern physics needs to be modified. If someone discovered the ultimate laws of physics five thousand years ago, coded those laws in the form of a sacred book, and made sure that not a single letter of that book would be altered in any way, then it is the duty of scientists to investigate this matter very seriously. We have seen that Vedic sages knew about electric force and electron, now we will see that they knew about electric charge, electricity and magnetic field as well.

"Nothing is too wonderful to be true."
- Michael Faraday

12. ELECTRICITY AND MAGNETISM

In Chapter six Indra was identified as electric force. If Vedic sages knew the existence of electric force, they must have had precise knowledge of related scientific phenomena. You are about to find out that the phenomena of electricity and magnetism have been described in detail in the Vedas. We will start by taking up the discussion of Soma, the drink of the gods.

12.1: Soma

The Ṛgveda is emphatic in saying that the real meaning of Soma is very different from the apparent meaning of a herbal plant, whose juice is supposed to be very intoxicating.

"When herb is crushed, people think they have drunk Soma. The Soma that wise people know, nobody can eat that." Ṛgveda 10.85.3

Soma has a very important place in the Ṛgveda. Ninth book of the Ṛgveda consisting of 114 hymns is solely dedicated to purifying Soma. Gods are invoked to drink the juice of Soma. Indra is often described in the Vedas as drinking the juice of Soma. The effect of drinking Soma is quite intoxicating on Indra. He performs great deeds under the influence of Soma. If Indra is electric force, Soma can be identified as electric charge. Electric force depends on the magnitude of the electric charge, greater the charge, greater the force. According to Ṛgveda 10.42.4 Indra does not befriend those who do not offer Soma. This is so because electric force can act between electrically charged particles only.

The relationship of Soma with fundamental particles is described in the Vedas. Following question is asked in Vedas:

"What is the semen of strong horse?" Ṛgveda 1.164.34, Yajurveda 23.61

Answer is provided in the next verse.

"Soma is the semen of strong horse." Ṛgveda 1.164.35, Yajurveda 23.62

It is noteworthy that Soma as a plant cannot be related to the semen of horse as an animal. The Vedas are full of such descriptions, which make no sense at all unless we realize what the Vedas are about. Here Soma is the electric charge and horse is Aśva particle. These verses are saying that electric charge is distributed all over Aśva particle. In Ṛgveda 1.28.9 and 9.65.25 Soma is said to be kept on cow's skin. In Ṛgveda 9.66.29 Soma is said to play on the skin of cow. This means that electric charge is distributed over the surface of Gau particle. Vedas make a difference about whether charge is distributed all over the particle or only on the surface. In modern physics such questions do not arise because fundamental particles are considered point particles. Another recurring theme in the Ṛgveda is that of purification of Soma by passage through hair of sheep (9.6.1, 9.20.1). This refers to passage of electric charge through field lines of Avi particle, but meaning of purification is not clear to me.

Soma lives on mountain (Ṛgveda 9.82.3). The name of this mountain is Muñjavāna. There is no mountain to be identified by this name. In the Vedas surface of the universe is called mountain. Matter and energy is created at the surface of the universe. As most of the matter particles are electrically charged, electric charge is also created at the surface. It is in this sense that Soma is said to live on the mountain. Outside of the universe is considered ten-dimensional in Vedas. In Ṛgveda 9.6.5 and 9.8.4, it is said that ten fingers take care of Soma. Ten women call Soma in Ṛgveda 9.56.3. The ten dimensions are represented as ten fingers or ten women and these verses represent creation at the surface of the universe.

12.2: Indu

In the Ṛgveda there are two related terms "Soma" and "Indu", both have come to mean moon in later literature. Another word for moon "Chandramā" also occurs in Ṛgveda, which is again used in a technical sense, because Chandramā is said to reside in waters. In the Ṛgveda, word Soma is used for the herbal plant and word Indu is used for its juice. Having identified Indra with electric force and Soma with electric charge, Indu can be identified with electricity. Electricity is the flow of electric charge, and when juice of Soma flows it is called Indu. Here is a beautiful hymn dedicated to Indu.

Ṛgveda 9.2

Sage: Medhātithi Kāṇva; Deity: Pavamāna Soma; Metre: Gāyatrī

1. Soma is very gratifying to the gods, pure and pleasing. Indu, enter in mighty Indra.
2. Indu possesses great strength and splendor. Give us those qualities. Upholder sit in Yajña.
3. The pious stream of Soma juice provides lovely honey. Performer of good deeds lives with water.

4. Great rivers carrying water come to you, mighty, when you are mixed with cows.
5. Who holds and keeps heaven and ocean apart, is mixed in water. Purified Soma comes to us.
6. Worthy of perception like great Mitra, strong Hari makes sound. He brightens by sun.
7. Indu, your praises purify, activate and provide strength, by which you brighten for happiness.
8. We ask you to encourage us. You inspire the world to work. Your glories are great.
9. Indu, you take us to Indra. Purify us by sweet streams, like rain producing clouds.
10. Indu, you provide cows, men, horses and food. You are the first soul of Yajña.

Verses three to five relate Soma to water. Water represents matter and anti-matter, and their association with Soma means that matter and antimatter are electrically charged. First half of verse three is the most important clue to another scientific phenomenon. It tells us that honey is provided by stream of Soma juice. Word for honey in Sanskrit is Madhu and Vedic literature is full of allusions to a hidden knowledge called Madhu Vidyā, knowledge of Madhu. This is the right time to discover the secret of Madhu Vidyā.

12.3: Madhu

It is well understood in Physics that phenomena of electricity and magnetism are interrelated. A moving electric charge gives rise to magnetic field. Stream of Soma juice is the movement of electric charge, and if it provides Madhu, then Madhu must be magnetic field. Now Madhu or honey tastes sweet, and it is for this reason that Madhu also means sweet. In Vedas almost everything in the universe is described as sweet or full of honey. Consider the following verses:

"Truthful air is sweet, rivers are flowing with honey. Herbs are full of honey for us." Ṛgveda 1.90.6

"Night and dawn are sweet, dust of earth is soaked with honey. Father heaven be sweet for us. Ṛgveda 1.90.7

"Vegetation be soaked with honey for us, sun be soaked with honey. Cows be full of honey for us. Ṛgveda 1.90.8

One verse from Upaniṣad says:

"This earth is the honey for all beings, and all beings are honey for earth." Bṛhadāraṇyaka Upaniṣad 2.5.1

These verses are telling us that magnetic field pervades almost everything in the universe. In Ṛgveda 2.10.2 Agni is called dispenser of honey. This signifies that magnetic field carries energy. Ṛgveda 7.47.2 says that waves of water are full of honey and Ṛgveda 10.30.13 describes waters as carrying honey. These verses describe the magnetic field generated by the movement of electrically charged particles. In Ṛgveda 1.90.8 sage prays for their cows to become full of sweetness. This verse describes the magnetic field around Gau particle.

Bṛhaddevatā 3.19-22 tells the following story about the secret knowledge of Madhu:

"Sage Dadhīchi knew the knowledge of Madhu. Indra told the sage not to mention the knowledge of honey to anyone, otherwise he will kill the sage. Aśvins asked the sage for the knowledge of honey and the sage expressed his inability quoting Indra's threat. Aśvins implored the sage to give the knowledge while having the shape of a horse-headed man. Upon his nod, Aśvins cut the head of the sage and joined the head of a horse to the body of the sage and received the knowledge of Madhu. When Indra came to know of this, he severed the head of horse from the sage. Aśvins joined the original head of the sage and revived him."

This story is based on Ṛgveda 1.116.12 and 10.48.2. These verses point towards an intimate connection between Madhu and Aśvins. It is time to investigate this connection and unravel the secret of Aśvins.

12.4: Aśvins

Aśvins are twin gods in the Vedas. They are always mentioned as a pair. One of them is called Nāsatya and other is called Dasra. Aśvins are considered physicians of the gods. In Greek mythology they are called Dioskauroi. In Avesta they are called Nāoṃhaithyā (Nāsatya) and are considered demons.

We have two important clues to figure out the secret of Aśvins. One, they are related to magnetic field and two, they are twins. Does something very familiar ring a bell? Of course, the magnetic poles. Aśvins are magnetic poles. Magnetic poles are always found as a pair. They can never be isolated. Let's see if our identification of Aśvins with magnetic poles finds further support in the Vedas.

Aśvins are called Madhuvarṇa, having color of honey, in Ṛgveda 8.26.6. In Ṛgveda 5.75 Aśvins are called Mādhvī, full of sweetness, in all nine verses. They are called Madhūyu, filled with honey, in Ṛgveda 5.73.8 and 5.74.9. In Ṛgveda 1.180.2 they are called Madhupa and in Ṛgveda 8.22.17 Madhupātama, both words meaning drinkers of honey. According to Ṛgveda 1.112.21 and 10.40.6, Aśvins provide honey to honeybees. His chariot is called Madhuvarṇa, having color of honey, in Ṛgveda 5.77.3. His chariot is also called Madhuvāhana, vehicle for carrying honey, in Ṛgveda 1.34.2, 1.157.3 and 10.41.2. They have a madhumatī kaśā, a whip soaked in honey, according to Ṛgveda 1.22.3 and 1.157.4. Obviously these descriptions describe a very intimate connection between Madhu and Aśvins. Anthropomorphic description of gods is the style of the Ṛgveda to convey abstruse scientific knowledge in a dramatic way. Here the connection between the magnetic field and the magnetic poles is so strong that Aśvins have been described as drinking honey, carrying honey, even having the color of honey. You will recall that a similar description of god Savitā is found in the Ṛgveda. Energy is described as golden in the Vedas, and therefore god Savitā has been described as having everything golden. Once we know the scientific meaning of the Vedas, then we realize that these descriptions are not arbitrary, but there is a remarkable precision in these representations.

There are forty one complete hymns dedicated to two Aśvins (1.34, 1.46-47, 1.112, 1.116-120, 1.157-158, 1.180-184, 2.39, 3.58, 4.43-45, 5.73-78, 6.62-63, 7.67-74, 10.39-41, 10.106, 10.143). Now is the perfect time to ponder over the scientific meaning of a mysterious hymn dedicated to twin gods Aśvins.

Ṛgveda 1.34

Sage: Hiraṇyastūpa Aṅgirasa, Deity: Aśvins,

Meter: Jagatī, 9,12 - Triṣṭupa

1. O learned, today be ours three times. O Aśvins, your chariot and gift are all-pervading. Like (warm) clothes are intimately connected with winter, you two come very near to wise people.

2. Chariot carrying honey has three tires. Your longing for Soma is well known. Three pillars are fixed on your chariot to give support. O Aśvins, you travel three times in night and three times a day.

3. O concealer of imperfection, today mix Yajña with honey three times in the same day. O two Aśvins, give us

strengthening food three times fully during morning and evening.

4. Come to our home three times. Go to your followers three times. Teach the three kinds of knowledge three times to good people. O two Aśvins, carry the pleasure providing materials three times and nourish us with permanent food three times.

5. O two Aśvins, carry the wealth three times, come to Yajña three times and protect our intellect three times. Give wealth three times and grains three times. Daughter of sun is now riding on your chariot with three wheels.

6. O Aśvins, give us the herbs from heaven three times, from earth three times and from waters three times. O lord of good fortune, for the protection and happiness of our children provide the threefold shelter.

7. O adorable Aśvins, sit down on our altar of threefold earth every day three times. O charioteer Aśvins, come to our homes three times even from faraway places like the life giving air.

8. O Aśvins, three containers have been filled three times by the seven mother rivers. Oblation is also divided in three. You protect three earths and the vault of heaven above day and night.

9. O Nāsatya, where are the three wheels of the chariot with three enclosures? Where are the three connections in the same place. When will the strong donkeys be yoked in your chariot riding which you come to the Yajña.

10. O Nāsatya, come here, where oblation is being offered. Drink sweet drinks by your mouths used to drinking honey. Savitā

instigates your beautiful chariot smeared with clarified butter even before dawn for Yajña.

11. O Nāsatya Aśvins, come here to drink honey with three times eleven gods. Make our lives prolonged, purify us by removing our weaknesses, remove jealousy and always stay with us.

12. O Aśvins, bring to us good warriors and wealth by your chariot of three enclosures. I call you hearers for our protection. May we expand in battles.

A special connection is made between Aśvins and number three in these verses. Three containers in verse eight are three spaces, earth, atmosphere and heaven. Meaning of invoking Aśvins to come three times every day will become clear later, when I discuss Vedic cosmology. For now we will focus our attention to another phenomenon deeply connected with electricity and magnetism, that of light.

"I do not know what I may appear to the world, but to myself I seem to have been only like a boy playing on the seashore, and diverting myself in now and then finding a smoother pebble or a prettier shell than ordinary, whilst the great ocean of truth lay all undiscovered before me."

- Isaac Newton

13. LET THERE BE LIGHT

When we think of light, our attention is immediately turned towards the sun or "Sūrya" in Sanskrit. Sūrya has a unique identity in the Ṛgveda and cannot be confused with other deities who have merged their identity in the sun of the post-vedic literature. As the Ṛgveda is a coded book, actual meaning of Sūrya is not sun in the Ṛgveda. Five complete hymns have been dedicated to Sūrya in the Ṛgveda (1.50, 1.115, 10.37, 10.158, and 10.170). There are eighteen other mantras dedicated to Sūrya in hymns dedicated to other gods (Ṛgveda 1.164.46-47, 4.40.5, 5.40.5, 7.60.1, 7.62.1-3, 7.63.1-5, 7.66.14-16, 8.101.11-12, and 10.139.1-3). Sūrya is time and again related to eyes in the Vedas.

"From his mind moon was born, from his eyes Sūrya was born." Ṛgveda 10.90.13

"O Sūrya, give our eyes the power to see." Ṛgveda 10.158.4, Atharvaveda 13.1.145

"Sūrya is the Lord of eyes." Atharvaveda 5.24.9

Even in the Brāhmaṇas identification of Sūrya with eyes continues, however at some places Sūrya starts to be substituted by other deities who have merged their identity in Sūrya.

"Sūrya is situated in my eyes." Taittirīya Brāhmaṇa 3.10.8.5

"Which is your eye, that is Āditya." Śatapatha Brāhmaṇa 10.3.3.7

The eyes are related to light, and that is exactly what the Vedas mean, when they talk about Sūrya. Considering that the Ṛgveda is a book of cosmology, it cannot mean sun by Sūrya, because sun has no special place in the cosmos. Sun is one out of billions of stars in cosmos, and the Ṛgveda in order to be consistent must deal with more fundamental properties of the universe. There are ample evidences to prove that Sūrya does not mean sun in the Ṛgveda. The Ṛgveda talks about several Sūryas in verses 9.114.3 and 10.88.18, while there can be hardly any doubt that the sun is only one.

Sūrya has been called "Urucakṣā" in Ṛgveda 7.35.8 and "Dūredṛśa" in Ṛgveda 10.37.1, both meaning seeing very far. Sūrya is also called "Viśvacakṣā" meaning seeing all in Ṛgveda 1.50.2. These descriptions fit very well with the identification of Sūrya with light.

Ṛgveda 1.115

Sage: Kutsa Āṅgirasa; Deity: Sūrya; Metre: Triṣṭupa

1. Eye of Mitra, Varuṇa and Agni and front army of gods has risen. He has pervaded heaven, earth and atmosphere. Sūrya is the soul of moving and unmoving.

2. Sūrya follows radiant goddess Uṣā like a man follows a beautiful woman, where men desiring to become god stretch time by good deeds for welfare of people.

3. Auspicious green horses of Sūrya are wonderful, pleasing and always moving. Venerable spread on the surface of heaven and immediately go round earth and heaven.

4. That is the glory and godliness of Sūrya that he pulls away his rays in the middle of actions. When he pulls away his green horses from the world, night spreads its cloth for him.

5. That Sūrya creates forms near heaven for observation of Mitra and Varuṇa. His green horses take two forms, one of infinite brightness and vigor, and other black.

6. O gods! Protect us from sins and blamable deeds when Sūrya is rising. Let Mitra, Varuṇa, Aditi, Sindhu, earth and heaven express approval for our statements.

In first verse Sūrya is called the eye of Mitra, Varuṇa and Agni. In Ṛgveda 7.63.1 also Sūrya is called the eye of Mitra and Varuṇa. Similar views are expressed in verse five quoted above as well. Mitra and Varuṇa have been identified with electron and proton earlier. How do protons and electrons find out what is around them? They continuously send signals all around them. These signals are electromagnetic waves, and light is also electromagnetic wave. It is in this sense that Sūrya is considered the eye of Mitra and Varuṇa. When this scientific meaning was forgotten, Sūrya, Mitra and Varuṇa along with many other gods came to mean just sun. In verse five, horses of Sūrya are said to take two forms, bright and black. These two forms are that of particle and anti-particle. The Ṛgveda calls particle form bright and anti-particle form black or dark.

The field properties of light are described in the Ṛgveda by calling Sūrya as Śociṣkeśa, having inflamed hair (1.50.8), or Keśina, having fine hair (1.164.44, 10.136.1) or Harikeśa, having green hair (10.37.9). Having inflamed hair signifies that field is another form of energy. Sūrya is described as having green hair and his chariot is also driven by green horses. Both of these descriptions describe same phenomenon, which has nothing to do with either hair or horses. Number of horses driving the chariot of Sūrya is seven.

Seven draw the chariot of Sūrya, one horse having seven names draws the chariot. Ṛgveda 1.164.2

"Seven horses draw the chariot of Sūrya" Ṛgveda 5.45.9

These seven horses are the seven colors comprising light. These seven colors become visible in a rainbow or when light passes through a prism. Green color was chosen to represent the light as green light falls in the middle of electromagnetic spectrum comprising seven colors of light.

In modern physics light is considered a wave as well as particle. Light particle is called photon. In Vedas Gau particle seems to be related to the concept of photon. Cows of sun are mentioned in Ṛgveda 7.36.1. This would mean Gau particles of light. Photons have a very special property. They are considered massless, meaning they do not have any rest mass. Yajurveda also has same opinion about Gau particle.

"What does not possess mass?" Yajurveda 23.47

"Cow does not possess mass." Yajurveda 23.48

Reader should note that these verses cannot apply to an animal called cow. The information in the Vedas is coded and only those who were familiar with the code could understand the meaning of the Vedas. The Vedic code was forgotten over time, but some part of the code was remembered up to the first half of second millennium. A very surprising piece of evidence has surfaced up recently. Professor Subhash Kak has discussed in a recent article the value of the speed of light as given by Sāyaṇa [1]. Sāyaṇa

(1315-1387 A.D.) was the prime minister in the court of Emperor Bukka I and his successors of the Vijayanagar empire. Sāyaṇa was a well known Vedic scholar. In his commentary on Ṛgveda 1.50.4, he says that sun (Sūrya) traverses 2,202 yojanas in half a nimeṣa. Yojana is an ancient Indian unit of length, and nimeṣa is a unit of time. Upon conversion into modern units, this yields the value of 186,000 miles per second. Thus Sāyaṇa was describing the speed of light, and not that of sun, following the Vedic tradition of the coding of knowledge.

How did light originate? Ṛgveda provides various clues:

"Gods took out Sūrya from ocean." Ṛgveda 10.72.7

"Indra created Sūrya." Ṛgveda 2.12.7

"Indra and Viṣṇu created Sūrya." Ṛgveda 7.99.4

"Sūrya was created by Uṣā." Ṛgveda 7.78.3

"Sun was born from Vṛtra." Atharvaveda 4.10.5

These verses are saying that light originated due to expansion of the universe by electric force. Ṛgveda is very clear that Sūrya resides in light space, and not in the observer space or intermediate space.

"Sūrya is son of heaven." Ṛgveda 10.37.1

"Indra and Soma established Sūrya above." Ṛgveda 6.72.2

It is for this reason that I have given the scientific name of heaven as light space. Energy has three principal forms in three spaces, Sūrya in heaven, Vāyu in atmosphere and Agni in earth. It is for this reason that Vāyu and Agni are called brothers of Sūrya in Ṛgveda 1.164.1. Sūrya is also very intimately associated with the goddess Uṣā. Ṛgveda 1.115.2 says that Sūrya follows Uṣā like a man follows a beautiful lady. We will take up the discussion of Uṣā next to understand the meaning of this mantra.

"I 'saw' cascades of energy coming down from outer space, in which particles were created and destroyed in rhythmic pulses; I 'saw' the atoms of the elements and those of my body participating in this cosmic dance of energy; I felt its rhythm and I 'heard' its sound, and at that moment I knew that this was the Dance of Śiva, the Lord of Dancers worshipped by Hindus."

- Fritjof Capra

14. THE DANCE OF CREATION

Two words for the world in Sanskrit are Jagata and Saṃsāra. Jagata means one that is continuously moving and Saṃsāra means one that is always flowing. It was well understood by the Vedic sages that everything in the universe is continually moving. So much is going on behind the scene. So many changes are taking place inside what looks like unchanging to us. The concept of two goddesses, Uṣā and Nakta, are related to the dynamics of changes unseen by us.

14.1: Uṣā (the dawn)

There are twenty complete hymns dedicated to Uṣā in Ṛgveda (1.48-49, 1.113, 1.123-124, 3.61, 4.51-52, 5.79-80, 6.64-65, 7.75-81, and 10.172). Hymns dedicated to Uṣā are subtle and beautiful. It is right time to go through a beautiful hymn dedicated to Uṣā.

Ṛgveda 1.123

Sage: Kakṣīvāna Dairghatamasa Auśija; Deity: Uṣā; Meter: Triṣṭupa

1. Grand right-handed chariot of Uṣā has been assembled and immortal gods have taken their seat on it. Leaving behind and rising from black darkness, kind Uṣā intends to provide dwelling for mankind.

2. She wakes up before the whole universe does. She wins riches and donates generously. First to be invoked Uṣā has come and the young lady, who takes birth again, has started watching from high place.

3. Well-born goddess Uṣā gives the share of wealth to mortal men today. Let dear god Savitā say here for Sūrya that we are sinless.

4. Every day she goes to every home and takes form. Wishing to obtain the oblations bright Uṣā always comes and procures the first riches.

5. First to be praised joyful Uṣā is sister of Bhaga and sibling of Varuṇa. Let's win by your right-handed chariot and the holder of sin be caught.

6. Songs of joy be told in abundance and fires be kindled. Let desirable wealth hidden in darkness be manifested by shining Uṣās.

7. One comes towards, other goes away. Having opposite forms they travel one after another. One covers everything in darkness, other manifests them by radiant chariot.

8. They are similar today and they will be similar tomorrow. They care for vast abode of Varuṇa. Each blemishless Uṣā goes round thirty yojanas instantly.

9. Knower of the name of the first part of the day, white pure Uṣā manifests from darkness. Young woman does not break the universal law and moves separating one day from another.

10. Like a lady revealing her body, Goddess goes to the God to fulfill wishes. Radiant lady shows her breasts in front of him smilingly.

11. Like a young lady adorned by mother, beautiful Uṣā shows her body. You noble lady keep shining up to far away places. Other Uṣās cannot compare to you.

12. Possessing cows and horses and chosen by all, they try to dispel darkness by sun's rays. Uṣās holding auspicious names, go far away and come back again.

13. O Uṣā, living in accordance with rays of cosmic order, give us the desire to perform noble work. Keep shining before us. Give wealth to us and rich people.

In verse two Uṣā is described as first to be invoked and in verse six Uṣā has been asked to manifest the wealth hidden in darkness. This wealth is not ordinary wealth, but the stuff that universe is made of. Everywhere in the universe the process of creation and annihilation of particles is going on all the time. New particles keep on taking the place of old ones, creating an illusion of permanency. Uṣā is the name for creation of particles. The process of creation starts with Uṣā and therefore she is the first to be invoked. Uṣā has been frequently described as showing her body in Ṛgveda. As Uṣā manifests the unmanifested, she is visualized as showing her body. Frequently more than one Uṣā is mentioned as in verse twelve. This is because many particles are being created simultaneously everywhere and particles have a very short life span. Tilak argues that Aryans lived in Arctic region before the diaspora based on the description of several dawns [1]. He argues that Arctic region has a very long dawn, which is described as being equivalent to many dawns of Indus valley. This argument is not very logical, as a long dawn will still be described as one dawn, not many dawns.

Uṣā shows her breasts like a dancer (Ṛgveda 1.92.4). Uṣā keeps her breasts open (Ṛgveda 6.64.2). Figure 14.1 shows a famous statue from Indus Valley known as the dancing girl. We can now be more specific than that. This figure is that of Uṣā. Uṣā has been described as a nude dancing girl in Ṛgveda, which is a perfect match with the figure. Also, the pose of the dancing girl is a classical Indian dance form.

In verse one and five word "dakṣināya" has been used as adjective of the chariot of Uṣā. Sātavalekara translates it as dexterous, which does not seem correct. Dakṣa means dėxterous, but word "dakṣiṇāya" is related to dakṣiṇa meaning right or south. This seems to be related to spin of particles. In the Ṛgveda Sūrya is often described as following Uṣā. This may represent emission of photon (light particle) accompanied by the creation of particles. As light is represented by sun in Vedas, this also gives us a clue as to why dawn was chosen to represent creation of particles. Uṣā is called Divoduhitā, daughter of heaven, in the Ṛgveda. This is because process of creation starts in the light space. There is a continuous interaction between light space and observer space with energy changing into particles and particles changing into energy.

Verse seven describes Uṣā and Nakta. Nakta is described as covering everything in darkness. We will take up the discussion of Nakta now to get further insight in the process of annihilation of particles.

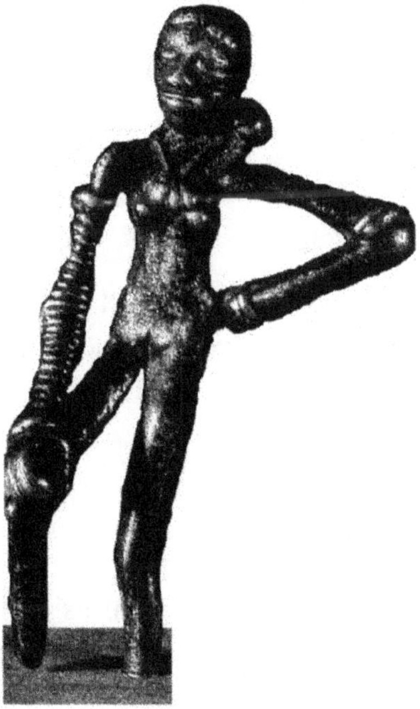

Figure 14.1: Uṣā, the dancer, a statue from Indus Valley

14.2: Nakta (the night)

Nakta means night, but that is not the intended meaning in the Vedas. Uṣā represents the creation of particles and therefore Nakta represents the annihilation of particles. It is time to further investigate if this interpretation is supported by the Vedas. In Yajurveda 23.11 following question is raised:

"What object is Pilippilā and what object is Piśaṅgilā?"

Pilippilā is something that is very soft and presses very easily. Piśaṅgilā means devourer. The answer is given in the next mantra.

"Avi is Pilippilā and night is Piśaṅgilā?" Yajurveda 23.12

Here Avi particle is described as soft and night is described as devouring all the forms. However, the inquirer is still curious and asks the question again to get a definite answer. Then he gets following answer.

"Aja is Piśaṅgilā, who like a dog gets things out and devours it again." Yajurveda 23.56

Here Aja particle is related to night as both are described as devourer. Reader should recall that Aja is the intermediate stage between manifestation of energy into matter particles and vice versa. Thus Aja creates forms as well as annihilates forms. In this way Aja is related to Uṣā and Nakta both. The relationship of Nakta with annihilation of particles is made clear in the following verse from Ṛgveda as well, where Nakta is related to Savitā.

"Night was created for the birth of Savitā." Ṛgveda 1.113.1

Savitā is the creation-annihilation energy of the particles, and as the annihilation energy Savitā is related to night. As with many other Vedic themes, the depiction of the cosmic dance of creation and annihilation went through changes during the age of the Purāṇas.

14.3: Lord of the dancers

Creation and annihilation of particles is a continuous process. Everywhere in the universe this process is going on. The Vedic sages envisaged this process as a cosmic dance of creation, and therefore Uṣā is represented as a dancer. In later Hinduism this dance of creation is represented by the cosmic dance of Lord Śiva. It is for this reason that Lord Śiva is also called Naṭarāja, the Lord of the dancers. This dance is the creation and annihilation of matter and anti-matter. Energy changes into a pair of matter and anti-matter particles and when a particles and its anti-particle collide, they change into energy. We will take up the production of a pair of matter and anti-matter particles in the next chapter.

"I believe that the discovery of particles and anti-particles by Dirac has changed our whole outlook on atomic physics."
- Heisenberg

15. PAIR PRODUCTION

Male and female species form a pair in animal kingdom. A similar relationship exists in the particle world. Particles are also formed in a pair. Our universe is dominated by a set of particles, which we call matter. The opposite pairs of these particles are called anti-particles and the set of these anti-particles is called anti-matter. When a particle meets its anti-particle, they annihilate and change into energy. Energy under certain conditions changes into a pair of particle and anti-particle. The Vedas describe the opposing nature of matter and anti-matter in several ways.

15.1: Matter and anti-matter

The Vedas describe matter and anti-matter as twins. This is indeed a perfect description, as particle and its anti-particle are born together from the same womb (energy). Sometimes these twins are described as both sisters and sometimes as one brother and other sister. As these descriptions are not of human beings, these analogies are valid.

"Two female twins manifest in various forms. Out of them, one is white and other is black. The black and white females are sisters. This is one of the great deeds of gods." Ṛgveda 3.55.11

Vedas describe matter as white and anti-matter as black. Universe consists of matter and anti-matter. A verse from the Ṛgveda describes the division of energy in these two forms.

"Those born together were divided in two forms." Ṛgveda 1.62.7

Opposite forms can have two meanings, matter and anti-matter, or positive and negative electric charge. A positively charged particle attracts a negatively charged particle. Following verse describes this phenomenon.

"Two women having opposite forms breastfeed each other's child." Ṛgveda 1.95.1

Our universe is matter dominated. If matter and anti-matter are created together in same amount, then we should find equal amount of anti-matter. Why is it that we don't find much evidence of anti-matter as far as we can observe. Are remote parts of the universe anti-matter dominated? Did matter and anti-matter somehow get segregated in different corners of the universe? Scientists do not think so. Scientists believe that when universe was very young, for some reason a small excess of matter over anti-matter was generated. As matter and anti-matter annihilated each other, this small excess remained, and that small excess is the matter of our universe. The Vedas take a different view. According to the Vedas matter and energy are constantly being created at the surface of the universe, and there is an imbalance in their creation. Matter and anti-matter continually annihilate each-other and the small excess of matter has accumulated over the age of the universe. Following verses describe the annihilation of anti-matter.

"Indra killed all the female servants of black origin." Ṛgveda 2.20.7

"Every day Indra removed half of the people, similar to other half but black in color, born in his house." Ṛgveda 6.47.21

Indra is considered responsible for killing of black people in the Ṛgveda. As matter and anti-matter are attracted towards each other due to opposite nature of electric charge resulting in annihilation, electric force is indeed responsible for this phenomenon. The Ṛgveda contains a beautiful dialogue between a particle and its anti-particle in tenth book. The particle is represented as a brother and its anti-particle as his twin sister.

15.2: Yama and Yamī

Yama is depicted as the god of death in the popular form of Hinduism. His form is very different in the Vedas.

Ṛgveda 10.10

Sage: 1,3,5,7,9,11,13 - Yamī, rest - Yama; Deity: 1,3,5,7,9,11,13 - Yama, rest - Yamī; Metre: Triṣṭupa, 13 - Virāṭasthānā

1. Yamī: I want to choose my friend (Yama) as my husband. He has entered the foaming ocean of youth. Now I am mature to give birth, and I want you to establish in my womb your father's grandson.

2. Yama: Your friend (Yama) does not want this kind of friendship, because own sister is not suitable (for marriage). Great brave sons of Asuras, who hold the heavens, see everything.

3. Yamī: Though for a mortal this friendship is unsuitable, the immortals do want this contact. You should fall in love with me, and join with my body as a virile husband.

4. Yama: We have never done this before. We speak truth, we never spoke lies. Gandharva and young woman in Āpaḥ are our navel, and we have close relationship.

5. Yamī: All-pervading Tvaṣṭā has made us couples in womb itself. No one can break his laws. Earth and Heaven know our relationship.

6. Yama: Who knows about the first day? Who has seen it? Who can tell? The abode of Mitra and Varuṇa has wide expanse. Why are you saying all this filled with imagination leading to downward fall?

7. Yamī: In Yamī desire has arisen for Yama to sleep with him at the same place. Like a wife joins her body with husband's, we should also do so. Let's work together like two wheels of a chariot.

8. Yama: The spies of gods who move around here, (they) don't stop anywhere, don't close their eyes even for a moment. Go with someone else and work together with him like two wheels of a chariot.

9. Yamī: Let the sun shine, days and nights fulfil our desires. Let's be couple like earth and heaven. Let Yamī become Yama's wife.

10. Yama: Those times will come later, when sisters will have unsuitable relationship with brothers. O beautiful, choose someone else as your husband, and hold him in your hands.

11. Yamī: What of the brother, whose sister is helpless. What of the sister, who cannot alleviate the pain of the brother. Caught with desires I am saying so much to you, join your body with my body.

12. Yama: I will not join my body with your body. Who sleeps with his sister, (people) call (him) sinner. Enjoy with someone else. O lucky, your brother does not desire this relationship.

13. Yamī: You are a coward. I could not fathom your mind and heart. Does someone else hug you like a creeping plant goes around a tree or a rope binds a horse?

14. Yama: Yamī, you should also hug someone else. Like a creeping plant goes around a tree, let that someone else also hug you. You should desire him, he should desire you, and you enjoy life with him.

Yama means twin, and here one of the twins is called Yama and other his sister Yamī. This beautiful dialogue, which is cited as prohibiting the union of siblings, is not about the illegitimate relationship at all. This is a dialogue between a particle and its anti-particle. If they join together, they will change into radiation and material universe will not evolve. Vedas are written from the viewpoint of an existing universe, and sages celebrate the important physical processes leading to the present state of universe. The stress here is that material universe has evolved due to one particle combining with another particle to generate a third particle and so on. This is why Yamī is told to join with someone else, not her own anti-particle. Verse two says that sons of Asuras see everything. Verse eight says that spies of gods don't stop anywhere and don't close their eyes even for a moment. Who are these sons of Asuras and spies of gods? In Vedas Varuṇa is often called Asura. Varuṇa has earlier been identified as electron. The spies of Varuṇa are often mentioned in Vedas.

"Nobody can deceive the spies of Varuṇa" Ṛgveda 6.67.5

"Varuṇa's spies see everything by their thousand eyes." Atharvaveda 4.16.4

The electron keeps on sending virtual particles all around it to find out about its neighbors. In this way electron keeps an eye on everything around it. These spies are called dogs in Ṛgveda.

In the Ṛgveda 1.24 there is a beautiful prayer by a virtual particle Śunaḥ Śepa to Varuṇa (electron) asking Varuṇa to free him. This prayer becomes the basis of a long story in Aitareya Brāhmaṇa 7.3.1-6. King Hariśchandra had one hundred wives, but he had no son. He prayed to Varuṇa for a son and promised to sacrifice him. Varuṇa granted his wish and soon his son Rohita was born. Varuṇa asked Hariśchandra to sacrifice his son Rohita. Hariśchandra said that an animal becomes eligible for sacrifice when it is ten days old. He would sacrifice Rohita when he became ten days old. Varuṇa said let it be so. When Rohita became ten days old, then Varuṇa reminded Hariśchandra again. Hariśchandra said that an animal is sacrificed when it has teeth. He would sacrifice Rohita when he had teeth. Varuṇa said let it be so. Varuṇa reminded Hariśchandra again after Rohita had teeth. Hariśchandra said that an animal is sacrificed when its first set of teeth fall. He would sacrifice Rohita when his teeth fell. Varuṇa said let it be so. Varuṇa kept reminding Hariśchandra and he kept postponing the sacrifice of his son Rohita. When Rohita came to know of his father's promise to sacrifice him, he left home and started living in a forest. Varuṇa became angry and inflicted Hariśchandra with dropsy disease. Upon hearing this Rohita wanted to return, but Indra stopped him several times. In the forest Rohita met sage Ajigarta dying from hunger and thirst. Ajigarta had three sons, Śunaḥ Puchchha, Śunaḥ Śepa and Śunolāṅgula. Rohita said that he would buy one of his sons for one hundred cows and sacrifice him to fulfil the promise made to Varuṇa. Ajigarta said that the eldest son is the dearest to him and his wife said that the youngest son is the dearest to her. So they sold Śunaḥ Śepa to Rohita. Varuṇa agreed to the sacrifice of Śunaḥ Śepa in place of Rohita. When nobody was found willing to tie Śunaḥ Śepa to a post for sacrifice, his selfish father Ajigarta agreed to do so for one hundred cows. Śunaḥ Śepa was tied to the post from head to toe. When nobody was found willing to sacrifice Śunaḥ Śepa, his selfish father Ajigarta agreed to do so for one hundred cows. At this point Śunaḥ Śepa started to pray to the gods by the mantras in Ṛgveda 1.24-30. Varuṇa became very happy to hear his prayers and released him.

In the post-vedic literature we find the development of minor themes of the Ṛgveda in long captivating tales. There is a beautiful dialogue between the spy of the gods and guardians of cows in the tenth book of Ṛgveda and this is the subject of further investigation.

15.3: Saramā and Paṇi

Paṇis are described as the mighty enemies of Indra. They are hiding the cows, which Indra desires to obtain. Indra sends Saramā to negotiate on his behalf.

Ṛgveda 10.108

Sage: 2, 4, 6, 8, 10, 11 – Devaśunī Saramā, rest - Paṇis; Deity: 2, 4, 6, 8, 10, 11 – Paṇis, rest - Devaśunī Saramā; Metre: Triṣṭupa

1. Paṇi: Saramā, you have come here with what desires? The road leading here is very long. What is your aim in this? How did you spend the night? How did you cross the rivers?

2. Saramā: I am the messenger of Indra, and I am roaming under his wishes. I want your great treasures. From the fear of all-transgressing (Indra), that (river) protected me. Thus I crossed the river.

3. Paṇi: O Saramā, what does Indra look like, what is his vision, you have come so far away becoming his messenger. (Paṇis talk among themselves) If (Saramā) becomes our friend, (we) uphold her, and let her become the owner of herds of cows.

4. Saramā: I don't know of him being beaten, he beats everyone, becoming whose messenger I have come from far away. O Paṇis, flowing deep currents can't hide him, you will certainly be lying on the ground killed by Indra.

5. Paṇi: O lucky Saramā, desiring these cows you have reached the edges of heaven, how can anyone let them go without a war? Our weapons are also very sharp.

6. Saramā: O Paṇis, you don't talk like good armies. Though (you) sinners' bodies can't be wounded, and the roads leading here are invincible, in either case Bṛhaspati won't let you live happily.

7. Paṇi: Our treasure is rooted in rock and is full of cows, horses and other riches. These great protector Paṇis protect these treasures. You have come to this suspenseful place in vain.

8. Saramā: Soma-drunk Navagva, Āṅgirasa and Ayāsya sages will come here. They will divide the cows. Therefore you should abandon these great-sounding talks.

9. Paṇi: O Saramā, looks like you have come here forced by gods. Let's make you our sister. Don't go back. O lucky, we will even give you a part of our cowherd.

10. Saramā: I don't know brotherhood or sisterhood. Indra and dreadful Āṅgirasa know that. They sent me desiring the cows, so I have come. Therefore go far away from here.

11. Saramā: O Paṇis, go far away from here. Cows go upward by Ṛta. Bṛhaspati, Soma, Grāvāṇa, Vipras and sages have come to know these very secretly hidden treasures.

Saramā is called Devaśunī meaning bitch of the gods in the Ṛgveda. If there is still any confusion left about Saramā being a dog, Ṛgveda 10.14.10 says that Sārmeya, children of Saramā, are two dogs with four eyes. Obviously, the dialogue is meaningless, if you don't know what the Vedas are about. Dogs cannot talk to human beings, but this has not prevented proponents of Aryan Invasion Theory to make a nice tale about the pastoral culture of Aryans. Cows of Aryans have been stolen by Paṇis. They send Saramā to find out about the stolen cows. She finds out the cows and asks Paṇis to part with them, but they refuse. Then Indra goes and recovers the cows. Actually this dialogue is not about cows and dogs.

First few verses tell that Saramā has traveled very far to find the cows, and in verse five it is made clear that she has reached all the way to the edge of heaven. The edge of heaven is the boundary of the universe. This phenomenon is taking place at the very edge of the universe. There is no indication in this dialogue that cows have been stolen by Paṇis. They own the cows and Indra, Bṛhaspati and other sages want those cows. Paṇis are very strong enemies. Reader should recall that forces of expansion and contraction are in a very delicate balance. Indra indeed has very strong enemies to defeat. Paṇis are hiding cows, horses and other riches in rocks. We have also seen that boundary of the universe is called mountain in the Vedas. What lies beyond this boundary is thus rooted in rock. Cows, horses and other riches that Saramā wants, have not manifested yet. They will, once the universe expands further, and therefore Bṛhaspati knows about the secretly hidden treasure. Cows and horses are the fundamental particles that will be created once the universe expands further. Thus we find that this dialogue between Saramā and Paṇis is another way of representing the creation of matter and energy due to expansion of the universe. This is the most crucial point of Vedic cosmology, and therefore it is told again and again in various ways. In this dialogue Saramā is made messenger of Indra. Electric force acts by the exchange of virtual particles, and thus virtual particles can be considered the forerunners of electric force. At this stage one question arises about Paṇis. Are they supposed to be the same as Vṛtra? The description of Paṇis and Vṛtra in Ṛgveda does not warrant this conclusion. Both are opposed to expansion of the universe. Vṛtra has been identified as surface tension of the universe, which opposes the expansion. Another force that opposes the expansion is the force of gravitation. Further research is needed to verify whether Paṇis represent the force of gravitation. Verse eight and eleven tell that sages are also involved in this cosmic game of creation. What is the role of sages? What do they represent? We will take up the discussion of the sages in the next chapter.

"Such, in outline, but even more purposeless, more void of meaning, is the world which science presents for our belief. Amid such a world, if anywhere, our ideals henceforward must find a home. All the labors of the ages, all the devotion, all the inspirations, all the brightness of human genius, are destined to extinction."

- Bertrand Russell

16. THE SEVEN SAGES

The verses of Vedas are preceded by the description of sages, deities and metres. There are two major definitions of the Vedic sages. Nirukta 2.11 says that sage is because of seeing. The verses have been realized by sages during deep meditation. On the other hand, Ṛgveda Sarvānukramaṇi 2.4 says that one who speaks the verse is the sage of that verse. By generalizing this definition, rivers, serpents and birds are considered sages as well, because dialogues have been spoken by them. It is obvious then that the actual sage of those verses is someone else who has chosen to make animals or inanimate objects speakers. There are several problems in accepting the given names of sages as the composer of the respective verses. Some verses are repeated in Vedas, and same verses are ascribed to different sages at different places. Many times more than one sage is associated with one verse. Sometimes the number of sages for same verse goes to hundred (Ṛgveda 9.66). In some cases it is obvious that the names of sages are not of actual people, but they are symbolic representations of the ideas conveyed by the mantras. For example verses of Yajurveda 34.1-6 end with "tanme manaḥ Śivasaṅkalpamastu" meaning let my mind be of good intentions. Sage of these verses is Śivasaṅkalpa meaning good intention. Sometimes gods themselves become sages for some verses. Agni is the sage as well as deity of Ṛgveda 10.140. Thus it stands to reason that the names of sages are symbolic. I am going to take an extreme position by stating that none of the sages mentioned in the Vedas were actual people. Actual sages have not left their names, and all of the names of sages found in Vedas have a precise scientific meaning. This means that Vasiṣṭha, Viśwāmitra and names of other famous sages are not names of actual people. If this is the case, then how are we going to find out the actual meaning of the sages? Our biggest clue is the name itself, because every word in the Vedas has an etymological meaning. Furthermore, there are descriptions of sages scattered in the Vedas. Hopefully, wise sages have left enough clues to make an unambiguous identification. With this objective in mind I will describe a beautiful hymn related to the birth of Vasiṣṭha.

16.1: Vasiṣṭha

Books two to eight of Ṛgveda are considered family books, as each book is written by a sage and his family members. Authors of these seven books of the Ṛgveda are known as seven sages. Seventh book of the Ṛgveda is written by Vasiṣṭha and his family members. A dialogue between Vasiṣṭha and his sons provides vital clues about the identification of sage Vasiṣṭha.

Ṛgveda 7.33

Sage: 1-9 – Maitrāvaruṇi Vasiṣṭha, 10-14 - sons of Vasiṣṭha;

Deity: 1-9 – sons of Vasiṣṭha or Indra, 10-14 – Vasiṣṭha;

Meter: Triṣṭupa

1. (Indra says) Whitish, having braided hair on right side, living wisely have pleased me. Rising from the seat I told men that Vasiṣṭhas don't go far from me.

2. Brought ferocious Indra, who drinks from Soma vessel, from very far away. Indra chose Vasiṣṭhas over Soma prepared by Vayata Pasdyumna.

3. Which Sindhu was crossed in this way? Which Bheda was killed in this way? O Vasiṣṭhas, in this way which Sudāsa did Indra protect by your hymns in the battle of ten kings?

4. O men, from your Brahma our forefathers get satisfaction, let the axles do not fail. O Vasiṣṭhas, hold strength in Indra by the loud sound in Śakkarī.

5. Thirsty, surrounded and seeking help, (Vasiṣṭhas) praised (Indra) in battle of ten kings like heaven. Indra heard the prayers of Vasiṣṭha and created wide region for Tṛtsus.

6. Like the rods for prodding cows, Bharatas were small and divided. Vasiṣṭha became the town of Tṛtsus, and Tṛtsus' settlement began to extend.

7. Three create seed in Bhuvanas, three are the offsprings of Ārya who stay in front of light. Three are the Dharmas which serve Uṣās, Vasiṣṭhas know them all.

8. O Vasiṣṭhas, your greatness is spread like sun's light, is deep like ocean, has speed like air. Your hymns cannot be matched by anyone.

9. From the knowledge of the mysteries of heart, they walk among thousand twigs. Weaving that enclosure by Yama, Vasiṣṭhas sit among the Apsarās.

10. O Vasiṣṭha, Mitra and Varuṇa saw you radiating electric light. That was your one birth when Agastya held you in place.

11. Vasiṣṭha, you are son of Mitra and Varuṇa. O Brāhmaṇa, you are born from the mind of Urvasī. By heavenly hymns drop (of semen) fell, all the gods held you in Lotus.

12. He has the knowledge of both. He gives thousands or everything. Weaving that enclosure by Yama, Vasiṣṭha was born from Apsarā.

13. Born in Satra, instigated by hymns (they) dropped seed in a vessel simultaneously. In the middle "Māna" manifested, from that sage Vasiṣṭha was born.

14. Offering verses, offering chants, carrying Grāvāṇa, he is speaking. Vasiṣṭha is coming. Offer him respect with warm feelings.

Vasiṣṭha means a place to live and is derived from root "Vas" meaning to live. In verse six, Vasiṣṭha is referred to as a town (Pura) for Tṛtsus. The question is what is the scale of Vasiṣṭha's extent? Is it atomic level or cosmological level? In first verse Vasiṣṭhas are described as having white color. White color has two possible connotations. It either represents matter as opposed to anti-matter, or it represents positive charge as opposed to negative charge. Here I will choose it to mean that Vasiṣṭhas are positively charged. Same verse also describes Vasiṣṭhas as having braided hair on right side. This could represent spin of atomic particles. Indra says that Vasiṣṭhas cannot go far from him, which means that being positively charged Vasiṣṭhas give rise to electric force, and thus Indra is always near them. Second verse enforces the idea of Vasiṣṭhas having electric charge by saying that Vasiṣṭhas carry Soma.

Verse three is a very important verse as it talks about the famous battle of Sudāsa and ten kings. Every historian believes it to be a historical battle, and many of them relate it to the victory of Aryans over Dravidians. This is simply nonsense, because Sudāsa means a good Dāsa, and Dāsas are supposed to be Dravidians. So if this was a battle, it would mean a victory of Dravidians over Aryans. However this was not a historical battle at all. The verse asks which Sudāsa was protected by Indra? Certainly Sudāsa cannot be a proper name if it is preceded by which.

Verses ten to thirteen are important in identifying Vasiṣṭha. Vasiṣṭha is born from Apsarā. Apsarā means flowing from Āpaḥ. Thus Apsarā means the electric field surrounding the charged particles. One of the Apsarās is Urvaśī, mother of Vasiṣṭha. Obviously Vedic scientists gave different names to electric fields associated with different charged particles. Verse eleven says that Mitra and Varuṇa are fathers of Vasiṣṭha. Full name of Vasiṣṭha is Maitrāvaruṇi Vasiṣṭha, where Maitrāvaruṇi means son of Mitra and Varuṇa. This is certainly impossible if Vasiṣṭha was a human sage. Having identified Mitra as proton, Varuṇa as electron and Vasiṣṭha as a place to live, it is tempting to identify Vasiṣṭha as atomic nucleus or atom. Atomic nucleus fits the description exactly as Vasiṣṭha has white color and atomic nucleus is positively charged. Urvaśī can then be identified as the electric field inside the atom. Māna is derived from root "mā" to measure. Creation of Vaśiṣṭha from Māna signifies that size of nucleus is not arbitrary, but well measured depending on the strength of atomic forces. Another important point is that Agastya holds Vasiṣṭha. As the reader will recall, Agastya means fixed, not moving. Atomic nucleus is also fixed relative to the electrons surrounding it. Nucleus is very heavy compared to electrons, and for this reason is very immobile compared to electrons. Thus I see a very good match between properties of Vasiṣṭha and atomic nucleus. Another strong corroboration comes from following prayers by sage Vasiṣṭha to Varuṇa:

"When will I be inside Varuṇa?" Ṛgveda 7.86.2

"We will live inside Varuṇa sinless." Ṛgveda 7.87.7

As the atomic nucleus is surrounded by electron cloud, these verses make exact sense. The prayers of Vasiṣṭha and his family are compiled in the seventh book of the Ṛgveda. One prominent feature of this book is that sages are asking for good and beautiful homes. If seven family books of the Ṛgveda are arranged according to some important chronological markers, then this book represents the era when atomic nuclei started to be formed.

The birth of Vasiṣṭha is a very important event in the Vedic cosmology, and it is not surprising that it is described on a seal from Indus Valley. Figure 16.1 shows this seal from Mohenjo-daro (M-1186). This seal is known as "fig-deity" seal. Seven human figurine in the bottom row represent the seven sages of the Ṛgveda. Human figurine inside the jar is sage Vasiṣṭha. According to Ṛgveda 7.33.13 Vasiṣṭha was born in a vessel. Human figurine outside the jar is sage Agastya. Ṛgveda 7.33.10 describes Agastya as holding Vasiṣṭha in place. Fish sign represents Mitra and Varuṇa. Mitra and Varuṇa oversee the universe without blinking their eyes, and fish is also known as keeping its eyes open even while sleeping.

In Puranas sage Viśwāmitra becomes a bitter rival of sage Vasiṣṭha. However, there is no rivalry between these sages in the Ṛgveda. Sage of the second book is Gṛtsamada Bhārgava Śaunaka. Gṛtsamada means wise and happy, Bhārgava is derived from root "Bhraj" to illuminate and Śaunaka means related to dog. Dog represents virtual particles in Vedas.

Figure 16.1: The birth of Vasiṣṭha,
a seal from Mohenjo-daro (M-1186)

Sage of the third book is Gāthina Viśwāmitra. Gāthina means singer and Viśwāmitra means friend of all. Sage of the fourth book is Vāmadeva Gautama. Vāma means lovely as well as left and Deva means god. Gau means cow and Tama means darkness. Sage of the fifth book is Atri. Atri means devourer, and is derived from root "Ad" to eat. Sage of the sixth book is Bharadwāja. Bharadwāja means carrying high speed or strength. Sage of the eighth book is Kaṇva. Kaṇva is derived from root "Kaṇ" meaning a minute particle. Further research is needed to understand the scientific meaning of these sages. Having discussed the meaning of sages, it is now time to take a closer look at the Vedic concept of deities.

"I want to know how God created this world. I am not interested in this or that phenomenon, in the spectrum of this or that element. I want to know His thoughts, the rest are details."

- Albert Einstein

17. THE GODS GALLERY

Hindus are often put on defensive by the followers of Semitic religions, who attack Hinduism for being polytheistic. Logically, monotheism has no superiority over polytheism. That being so, it should be kept in mind that Hindus worship different gods only as a manifestation of one god in different forms. Hinduism is a religion of symbols, and each symbol has a specific meaning. So far we have found the scientific meaning of several gods described in the Vedas. Vedas describe the universe to be divided in three spaces, and accordingly gods also have a specific place in the universe.

17.1: Three-fold division

Though a large number of gods are described in the Vedas, it was well understood that gods are essentially three, one belonging to each space.

"There are three gods: Agni in earth, Vāyu or Indra in atmosphere and Sūrya in heaven. Each one of them is known by various names depending on the different actions performed." Nirukta 7.5

"There are three gods: Agni in earth, Vāyu in atmosphere and Sūrya in heaven." Kātyāyana in Sarvānukramaṇi 2.8

This view finds support from the following verse in the Ṛgveda itself.

"Let Sūrya protect us from enemies in heaven, Vāyu in atmosphere and Agni in earth." Ṛgveda 10.158.1

These three gods are three major forms of energy, as matter in observer space, field in intermediate space and light in light space. Apart from this three-fold division of the gods, Vedas also talk about thirty three gods.

17.2: Thirty three gods

Sometimes Hindus are ridiculed for worshipping 330 million gods. The source of this misconception is the description of thirty three gods in Vedas.

"Thirty three gods take part in Yajña." Ṛgveda 1.139.11

"Three more than thirty gods came to Yajña, knew our desires, and gave us two kinds of wealth." Ṛgveda 8.28.1

"O three plus thirty gods, you are worthy of praise." Ṛgveda 8.30.2

Who are these thirty three gods? The Vedas do not provide the names of these gods. In Śatapatha Brāhmaṇa 14.6.9.3 they have been described as eight Vasus, twelve Ādityas, eleven Rudras, Indra and Prajāpati. This is definitely wrong and shows the loss of knowledge of the Vedic science. The Vedas are very clear about the division of gods.

"O Aśvins, come here to drink honey with three times eleven gods." Ṛgveda 1.34.11

"There are eleven gods in heaven, eleven gods in atmosphere, and eleven gods in earth." Yajurveda 7.19

Thus the description of thirty three gods has to satisfy the criteria of placing eleven gods in each of the three spaces, and obviously the Śatapatha Brāhmaṇa fails there. It seems that the concept of thirty three gods is related to the geometry of the universe. In Purāṇas a massive mix up took place. The Vedas describe gods of thirty three types (Koṭi). Koṭi has additional meaning of ten million. Due to this mix up in two meanings of Koṭi, number of gods suddenly jumped from thirty three to 330 million.

17.3: The age of Purāṇas

During the age of Purāṇas, massive upheaval took place in the depiction of Gods. The Purāṇas were written for the masses. On one hand the Purāṇas had to remain faithful to the Vedas, and on the other hand they had to keep ordinary people interested in Dharma. As a result the science of the Vedas was given the form of long engrossing tales of fight between gods and demons. Viṣṇu took the place of supreme Godhead. Indra became his subordinate, and most of the time he had to worry about saving his kingdom from demons. Often demons became too powerful and expelled Indra and other gods from heaven. Vedic god Rudra now became Śiva. Five gods attained prominence during this period: Viṣṇu, Śiva, Śakti, Sūrya and Gaṇeśa. Accordingly there were five main sects of Hindus, Vaiṣṇava, Śaiva, Śākta, Saura and Gāṇapatya. Gradually Gāṇapatya merged with Śaiva, and Saura merged with Vaiṣṇava leaving only three prominent sects Vaiṣṇava, Śaiva and Śākta. The process of coding of the knowledge started by the Vedas continued in the age of Purāṇas. One example of this coding is the story of ten incarnations of Lord Viṣṇu.

17.4: Incarnations of Viṣṇu

The names of ten incarnations of Viṣṇu are given in Mahābhārata Śānti Parva.

"Matsyaḥ Kurmo Varāhaśca Nārsiṃho atha Vāmanaḥ.

Rāmo Rāmaśca Rāmaśca Kṛṣṇaḥ Kalkīti te daśa."

Ten incarnations in chronological order are fish (Matsya), tortoise (Kurma), boar (Varāha), half man-half lion (Nārsiṃha), dwarf (Vāmana), Rāma, Rāma, Rāma, Kṛṣṇa and Kalki. Three Rāmas in chronological order are Paraśurāma, Rāma and Balarāma. Ten incarnations of Lord Viṣṇu tell the story of evolution and therefore it is important to keep them in chronological order. First incarnation is fish, which lives in water. Fish incarnation corresponds to the beginning of life in water. Second incarnation is tortoise, which can live in water and on land as well. Tortoise incarnation represents the transition of life from water to land. Third incarnation is boar, which lives on land. At this stage transition from water to land is complete. Next incarnation is half man-half lion representing the evolution of life forms with higher intelligence than previous ones, somewhere in between lower animals and man. Fifth incarnation is dwarf incarnation. This is the stage of primates, who have not yet learnt to stand erect. Sixth incarnation is that of Paraśurāma. Paraśu means an axe and Paraśurāma is depicted as holding an axe. This represents the primitive man of stone age who is using stone tools for hunting. Next incarnation is that of Lord Rāma, who is represented as carrying bow and arrow. Now the human being is further down the road of civilization and using bow and arrow for hunting. Eighth incarnation is that of Balarāma, who is represented as carrying plough on his shoulder. Now the man has settled down and is using agriculture for sustenance. Ninth incarnation is that of Kṛṣṇa representing modern man. Tenth incarnation is that of yet to come Kalki. Kalki represents the future evolution of mankind. When Darwin proposed the theory of evolution, it was opposed tooth and nail by Church, and orthodox Christians still do not believe in evolution. In stark contrast to revealed religions, Hinduism has never indulged in suffocation of scientific thought. Instead it has incorporated science in religion. Hinduism has been developed by intellectuals, who have coded the information for everyone to follow. While common Hindus follow their religion without knowing the real meaning behind the myths and customs, it is expected that Hindu intellectuals would know and preserve the scientific meaning for posterity. Unfortunately, a lot of scientific understanding has been lost due to a millennium of foreign rule. It is the duty of educated Hindus to rediscover the lost knowledge and bring back the glory of Hinduism. Hinduism is not a set of mumbo-jumbo supposed to be delivered to a chosen fellow by God, but it is a result of concerted effort of generations of intellectual sages to discover the nature of ultimate reality. Sages deified scientific phenomena and Hindus are worshippers of science. To illustrate this point further, let's go to a city in central India, where Hindus come from all over India to worship time god.

17.5: The legend of Vikramāditya

Ujjain is a city in the state of Madhya Pradeśa. The city of Ujjain was once ruled by the legendary king Vikramāditya. King Vikramāditya was known for his valor and impeccable justice. His court was adorned by nine famous courtiers called Navaratna (nine gems), who were great scholars in different fields of knowledge. Despite extensive effort, Vikramāditya cannot be identified with any known historical king. Ujjain is famous for the temple of Mahākāla. There is no other temple in India, where Mahākāla is worshipped.

Is there a meaning behind the legend of Vikramāditya and worship of Mahākāla? The real meaning is revealed by considering the meaning of these words. Vikramāditya is made by joining prefix "Vi" to words "Krama" and "Āditya". "Krama" means order, "Āditya" means sun and prefix "Vi" means deviation. Therefore, etymologically Vikramāditya means the change in the course of sun. What is significant is that Ujjain is located on the tropic of cancer. Thus, sun comes to Ujjain during its northward journey, changes its course, and starts its southward journey. Vikramāditya is sun itself changing its course at Ujjain. Nine gems in the court of Vikramāditya are nine planets of the Solar system. Mahākāla is made by joining words Mahā, great, and Kāla, time. Thus Mahākāla means Time the great. Ujjain was known as Ujjayinī in ancient times and was the capital of ancient Avanti empire. Ujjayinī was center of Indian civilization for several centuries and famous for its astronomical observatory. Ujjayinī was equivalent of Greenwich, from where time was synchronized all over India and even abroad. New day commenced when it was six A.M. in Ujjayinī. When it is six in the morning in Ujjain, it is midnight in Britain. It is from this ancient system of changing date in the morning in Ujjain that changing date at midnight has been arrived at. It is little strange to change the date when everyone is sleeping. As time was synchronized in a large part of the world according to Ujjayinī standard time, it was only natural to designate the god of Ujjain as god time himself, and therefore the name Mahākāla, Time the great. Mahākāla is often identified with Lord Śiva, but there are no strong reasons to do so.

The spirit of Hinduism is logic and skepticism, and with this skepticism in mind we are going to take a closer look at the most accepted model of the universe, the Big Bang model.

"I can live with doubt and uncertainty. I think it's much more interesting to live not knowing than to have answers which might be wrong."
- Richard Feynman

18: DID BIG BANG HAPPEN?

Every ancient civilization believed in an egg-shaped universe, which was based on the Vedic cosmology. Later due to the confusion of Pṛthivī (observer space) with earth a geocentric model of the universe developed. With Christianity adopting this idea, earth and human beings received a favorite place in God's scheme of things. Church not only believed in these ideas, but persecuted anyone who dared to speak against these ideas. Following the rise of Church to power a long dark age commenced. Modern science had a difficult birth in the cradle of Christianity. Scientists were persecuted and burnt for formulating scientific theories, which Church perceived to be against its theory of creation. It is not a coincidence that modern science is against the idea of God and anything special about earth and human beings. In India this type of conflict never arose. Hinduism was raised on the foundation of science and freedom of inquiry. There is not a single incident of a scientist being persecuted by religious authorities in ancient India.

The challenge to Geocentric cosmology came in 1543, when Copernicus made a bold proposition that earth may not be at the center of the universe and may be rotating around Sun. Science never looked back after that. Kepler developed the idea further, based on which Newton developed the theory of gravitation. In 1915 Einstein generalized the theory of gravitation and provided the framework of modern cosmologies. In 1929 Hubble published his results describing the recession of galaxies. Hubble observed a simple relation between the recession velocity of a galaxy and its distance from earth. The day of Big Bang Cosmology had arrived.

18.1: The Big Bang Cosmology

In the Big Bang model the universe starts with a gigantic explosion, before which all the mass-energy of the universe was concentrated in a point of singularity. Space was created with this explosion which is expanding according to Hubble's law. Hubble's law states that recession velocity of a galaxy relative to another galaxy is proportional to the distance separating them. There is an implicit assumption that the universe is same in all direction. The universe is symmetric around each point in the universe, and it looks same from anywhere in the universe. There are no edges of the universe and there is no center of the universe in this model. This is illustrated by means of an expanding balloon. The universe is considered a four-dimensional analogue of the surface of a balloon, on which each point is moving away from other point. Big Bang model of the universe is illustrated in Figure 18.1. The universe is a four-dimensional analogue of the surface of a sphere. There is no inside or outside of this surface as this surface is all that exists.

How did scientists figure out that universe is like the surface of a sphere? We find the answer in the bible of cosmology, Gravitation [1]. Prevailing scientific wisdom demands from the universe that it be of uniform density, isotropic and closed. First two requirements mean that universe should be same everywhere and third requirement means that universe should have no boundary. The surface of a sphere satisfies all these requirements.

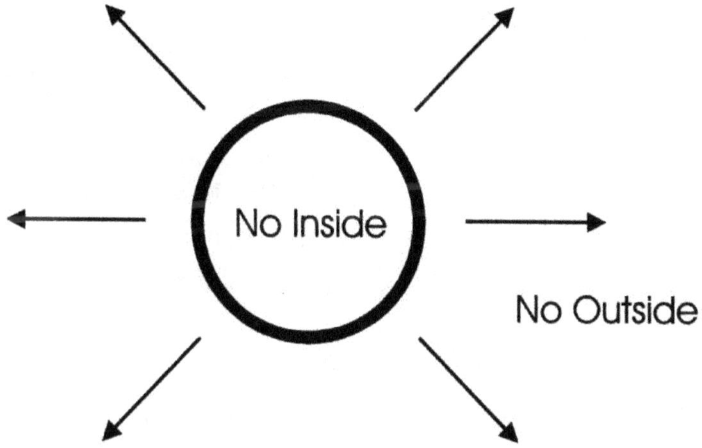

Figure 18.1: The Big Bang model of the universe

The questions like "What is inside the sphere" and "What is outside the sphere" are considered meaningless as the surface of the sphere is the whole universe, and there is no outside or inside. The bible of cosmology further says that excursion off the sphere is physically meaningless and is forbidden. We should note that it is one thing to demand from the universe to be what scientists consider elegant, and it is another thing for the universe to oblige the scientists by being so. The ultimate test for any theory of cosmology is the universe itself. Any theory must not contradict the universe, and we will see shortly that Big Bang Cosmology has failed in several respects. Failures of Big Bang Cosmology were apparent from the beginning itself, and soon after its birth another rival cosmology was developed to explain the universe better.

18.2: The Steady State Cosmology

In 1948 a rival cosmology named Steady State Cosmology was formulated by Hermann Bondi, Fred Hoyle and Thomas Gold. Steady State Cosmology differed from Big Bang Cosmology in several respects. Universe is considered without a beginning and a small amount of matter (hydrogen atom to maintain charge neutrality) is assumed to be created continuously between the galaxies. Universe is considered expanding in both models and looks same from every point in the universe. The important difference being that in Big Bang Cosmology Universe keeps changing with time as it is growing bigger, while in Steady State Cosmology Universe is always the same, presumably an infinite universe expanding and remaining infinite. For nearly two decades the controversy raged on and finally in 1965 scientific opinion turned in the favor of Big Bang Cosmology after the discovery of the cosmic background radiation.

Currently the Big Bang model is the most widely accepted model of the evolution of the universe. However, Big Bang model has a number of difficulties, some of which are supposed to be overcome using inflation like flatness and horizon problems. Some difficulties still remain like problems of singularity, dark matter, antimatter, the age of universe, the evolution of the galaxies, monopole, entropy, and rotation. Let's have a look at these problems.

18.3: The singularity problem

The Big Bang model is based on the observation that the universe is expanding. If we look backward in time, then universe will look smaller in extent, and if we extrapolate it all the way to the beginning of the universe, then universe will become a point. What happens to the mass-energy of the universe? One of the most sacred principles of physics is that mass-energy is always conserved. Mass-energy can neither be created nor be destroyed. The conservation principle then demands that in the beginning all the mass-energy of the universe was concentrated in a point. This point is called a singularity because its mass-energy density is infinite. In the Big Bang model there is a singularity at the beginning of the universe, and if there is sufficient mass-energy to close the universe, universe will end in another singularity. Though scientists don't like singularities, there is no way to avoid it currently. Scientists hope that a unified theory of quantum mechanics and gravity will be able to solve the singularity problem. The attempts to avoid the singularity at the beginning of universe have not been successful so far.

18.4: The horizon problem

The horizon problem was pointed out by Misner in 1969 [2]. The problem is related to causal connectivity. According to relativity no signal can travel faster than the speed of light. The universe is about 15 billion years old according to modern physics, so we have a horizon around us of 15 billion light years. We cannot receive any signal from a point beyond this horizon. If we look at an object 10 billion light years away, and then look at another object 10 billion light years away in the opposite direction, we find that they have similar environment. They have same expansion rate and same cosmic background radiation temperature. These two objects are however separated by a distance of 20 billion light years meaning that they are beyond the horizons of each other. Thus no signal has ever reached from one to the other. In the language of modern science these two objects have never been causally connected. How did the regions in space not causally connected get homogenized? If the universe started with a gigantic explosion, parts of it should show randomness characteristic of an explosion. Why is the universe so uniform then? This is the question posed by the Horizon problem.

An idea called "inflation" is used to find a way out of this problem and the Big Bang models using this idea are called the Inflationary Big Bang models. According to the inflationary model, universe started with the Big Bang, which made universe chaotic and inhomogeneous, but it was smoothed out later. Inflation is used to provide this smoothening effect in the Big Bang model. It should be kept in mind that there is no proof that inflation ever happened. The inflation theory cannot be tested.

18.5: The flatness problem

The flatness problem was pointed out by Dicke in 1969 [2]. It is related to omega, the ratio of average density of matter in the universe to critical density. The average density of matter is what is observed, and the critical density of the matter is the density needed to close the universe. If the density of matter is greater than the critical density, the universe will not keep expanding for ever, instead it will start contracting after a certain time, and universe will finish in a point of singularity. The measured value of omega is close to one. The problem is that, as the universe is between 10-20 billion years old in the Big-Bang model, the omega at Big Bang must have been very close to one, up to 59 decimal points! We can understand the Flatness problem by an analogy of a stone thrown in space from earth. If the stone has sufficient kinetic energy, it will escape the gravitational pull of earth and will never come back. If the stone does not have sufficient kinetic energy, it will fall back on earth. Important point here is that kinetic energy and potential energy keep changing with time. In first case ratio of potential energy to kinetic energy becomes zero, and in the later case it becomes infinity. Omega can also be defined as the ratio of potential energy to the kinetic energy. If omega were even slightly greater than or less than one, by now omega would be either close to zero or infinity. If omega were slightly greater than one, universe would have collapsed long time back. If it is close to one now, it has always been close to one, but why would the universe start with the value of omega so close to one. After all science does not believe in God who would set the value of Omega to exactly one. Inflation is used to solve this problem. Inflation drives omega to one regardless of its value before inflation takes place.

18.6: The age problem

The age of the universe lies between 7 and 20 billion years depending on the value of Hubble constant and other factors. The value of Hubble constant itself is a matter of raging controversy. The age of oldest stars is between 13 and 17 billion years. The age of the elements is between 12 to 16 years. This brings a peculiar situation that universe may be younger than its constituents. Physicists favor the lowest value of the Hubble constant to avoid the age problem. However, there is no scientific basis for this preference.

18.7: The monopole problem

Electricity and magnetism are intimately connected. Positive and negative electric charges are examples of electric monopoles, which can exist independently. On the other hand, magnetic monopole does not exist. A magnet always has a south pole associated with a north pole. If you cut a magnet in two, you end up having two magnets, each magnet having two poles. Why it is that electric monopole can exist, but magnetic monopole cannot? Are magnetic monopoles forbidden by nature? Scientists do not think so. Grand unified theories in conjunction with the Big Bang model predict the existence of magnetic monopoles. The mass of the monopole should be approximately ten million billion billion times that of the proton. New inflation theory predicts that there are many universes like several bubbles, and each universe contains one monopole. No monopoles have been found. If monopoles should exist, why are not they found? This is the question posed by the monopole problem.

18.8: The entropy problem

The entropy problem was formulated by Roger Penrose in 1974 [2]. Entropy is a measure of disorder. Second law of thermodynamics tells us that the entropy of the universe always keeps on increasing. If the universe started with a Big Bang, entropy of the universe should be much larger than it is observed right now. According to Penrose, the entropy in the early universe was extremely low. Universe began as an extremely ordered system. This is in direct contradiction with the Big Bang model according to which the universe began with a gigantic explosion and therefore the universe was very chaotic in the beginning.

18.9: The antimatter problem

As matter and antimatter are created and annihilated in pair. For every particle there exists an anti-particle, and when they come in contact, they annihilate each other. According to the standard Big Bang model, there should be same amount of matter and antimatter in the universe. However, our universe seems to be matter-dominated. Where is the corresponding anti-matter? Are there other galaxies made of antimatter in far recesses of the universe? Scientists have found no evidence of antimatter-dominated regions in universe. Why is it that in a supposedly symmetric universe distribution of matter and antimatter is asymmetric?

Considering that Big Bang model has been in existence for 70 years, and so many brilliant scientists have worked to solve these problems, why is it that the problems facing the Big Bang model refuse to go away? Is the framework of Big Bang model correct? The question to ask then is if not the Big Bang then what? Is there an alternative to Big Bang? Only serious challenger to the Big Bang model is the Steady State model, which has fallen out of favor after the discovery of the cosmic background radiation. In next chapter we will deliberate if the problems facing the Big Bang Cosmology can be solved by the Vedic Cosmology.

"We shall not cease from exploration
And the end of all our exploring
Will be to arrive where we started
And know the place for the first time."
- T. S. Eliot

19. THE VEDIC COSMOLOGY

So far in this book we have come across the cosmic egg several times. We know that the Vedic sages considered the universe to be egg-shaped and all ancient civilizations accepted the Vedic wisdom. Now is the time to deliberate why did the wise sages choose an egg to represent the universe? Was it because of a homely feeling or was there a solid reasoning behind this? Did sages look at the universe from outside? This is an unlikely scenario. In most likelihood they came to this conclusion based on sound reasoning.

19.1: The cosmic egg

We have seen that modern scientists consider the universe to resemble the surface of a sphere, because they have reasons to believe that the universe is isotropic, closed and curved. What considerations led the sages to the representation of the universe as an egg? The answer to this question lies in the rotation of the universe. We have a clear statement to this effect in the Ṛgveda.

"Which was born first and which later? How were they born? Who knows O wise people? They hold the universe by their strength and always keep rotating like a wheel." Ṛgveda 1.185.1

This mantra dedicated to observer space and light space clearly states them as rotating. As the universe is the sum of two, universe is also rotating. We have come across the notion that sages considered the universe to contain a primordial fluid, which they named "Salila". As apparent meaning of Salila is water, rest of the world came to believe that universe was filled with water in the beginning. If the sages considered the initial state of the universe to be a fluid, and they considered the universe to be rotating, the rotation will have an effect on the shape of the universe. If we rotate a spherical volume of fluid, the fluid takes the shape of a spheroid. It shrinks along the axis of rotation and expands perpendicular to it keeping its symmetry around the axis of rotation. If we look at a spheroid and think about a familiar object that looks like it, what do we come up with: surprise of surprises, an egg!!!

19.2: The chakra of Viṣṇu

In Hindu mythology, Lord Viṣṇu is shown as holding a chakra (wheel) in his hand. I have identified Viṣṇu as the universe, and that makes him same as Supreme Being, because in Hinduism God is not different from the universe. Now we can understand the symbolism behind the chakra. Chakra is the representation of the rotation of the universe. Lord Viṣṇu is shown as having four hands. The four hidden dimensions of the universe are his four hands. Now we may ask, if the universe is rotating, will not the scientists know about it?

19.3: Rotation of the universe

Almost everything in the universe is rotating including the particles, earth and galaxies. It is natural to ask if the universe is rotating as well. In the framework of the standard Big Bang model the universe is not rotating and this creates a problem as to why its constituents are rotating. The Big Bang model considers the universe to be isotropic, meaning there is no preferred direction in space. If universe is rotating, then it has an axis, which is a preferred direction. So finding a proof of the rotation of the universe is the end of the Big Bang model. Let's examine the assumption of isotropy carefully. If the universe is isotropic, there cannot be any distinction between left and right. This was the most sacred belief of scientists till 1956. That year two young scientists Tsung-Dao Lee and Chen Ning Yang published a scientific paper in which they claimed that parity, a measure of symmetry, might not be conserved in weak interactions. They proposed an experiment to test their hypothesis. There was an atmosphere of disbelief. Famous physicist Wolfgang Pauli, Nobel Laureate, known for his exclusion principle wrote a letter saying that he did not believe that the Lord is a weak left-hander. The experiment was conducted by a female physicist Chien Shung Wu a few months later and confirmed the argument of Lee and Yang. In 1957 Lee and Yang were awarded Nobel prize in physics for their discovery, and Wu received Wolf prize in Physics in 1978. Since then every experiment has confirmed that weak interaction makes a difference between left and right.

Let's take a close look at strong, electromagnetic and weak interactions. It is obvious that the model of the universe should not contradict the nature of these interactions. Weak interaction has complete disregard for many conservation laws including parity. Parity violation means that nature distinguishes between left and right. The question is how can this happen in an isotropic universe?

Let's ask another question: What is so special about weak interaction? Why is it that it does not obey conservation laws like other interactions? There indeed is something very special about weak interaction: its range of interaction. The range of electromagnetic and gravitational interaction is infinite. The range of strong interaction is 10^{-15} meters and that of weak interaction is 10^{-17} meters. Weak interaction has the lowest range of all interactions. We can think of weak interaction as operating at such a subtle level where the rotation of the universe affects the conservation laws. It has been more than forty years since the discovery of parity violation, but cosmologists have not taken into account what particle physicists have proved. This is obviously an indirect proof of the rotation of universe. Should not there be a more direct proof of this? Will not it be obvious if the universe were rotating? Well, earth is also rotating, but we do not feel it. We will have to look for the effect of this rotation. If the universe is rotating, it can be rotating very slowly as the universe is huge. In the beginning it may have been rotating faster. So is there a more direct proof of rotation of the universe? It turns out that we are just in luck.

Borge Nodland of the University of Rochester and John P. Ralston of the University of Kansas have found evidence of preferred direction in the universe and published their results in Physical Review Letters [1]. Scientific American, July 97 published a one page report on their findings under the heading "Science and the Citizen". After three years of painstaking research, Nodland and Ralston have found that polarized light from galaxies shows evidence of rotation. The twisting of polarized light is a well known phenomenon called Faraday effect. However, this rotational effect is on top of Faraday effect and depends not only on the distance of the galaxy from us, but it depends upon the direction of galaxy as well. The rotational effect is strongest in the direction of earth-Sextans axis and is weakest in the direction perpendicular to it. Nodland and Ralston have ruled out the possibility that the effect is local. The effect is at a cosmological level as it depends upon the distance of the galaxy.

The work of Nodland and Ralston has been challenged by other scientists, who think that the analysis is wrong. This is only expected as physicists are not going to abandon one of their most cherished beliefs so easily. It must be backed up by further evidence. Meanwhile Nodland and Ralston have maintained the position that their analysis is correct. They have stated that their result cannot be explained by conventional physics and the effect may be due to an unknown force or field or property of space. To me it is a direct proof of the rotation of the universe. The rotation of universe and continuous creation of matter and energy are two salient features of the Vedic cosmology. We have seen that universe has the shape of an egg due to rotation, now is the time to discuss continuous creation, which will lead us to a way out of singularity.

19.4: The universe without singularity

The universe started with an explosion according to the Big Bang model. At time equal to zero, all the mass-energy of the universe was concentrated in a point. This is certainly an unimaginable feat, as the universe is immense. According to Pauli's exclusion principle not even two electrons can occupy the same state, and here the whole universe is considered to be inside a point. The Big Bang model does not give any clue as to why all the mass-energy of the universe should be there in the first place. This situation is a direct result of the conservation of mass and energy, the most sacred principle of physics. Considering that the universe is expanding, extrapolating backward in time, the universe was as small as a point. As mass-energy of the universe must be conserved, all the mass-energy must have been there at time zero as well. We should note that the conservation of mass-energy is violated in this case as well. This is equivalent to saying that all the mass-energy was created at time equal to zero. Mass-energy density of the universe was infinite at time equal to zero, which is called a point of singularity.

Scientists have been trying to find a way out of singularity. Ed Tryon published a paper in Nature, December 1973 with the title "Is the universe a vacuum fluctuation?" Tryon, wondering about where all the mass-energy of the universe came from, proposed that it is due to a vacuum fluctuation. Uncertainty principle allows for creation of energy for a brief period of time. However, mass-energy of the universe being so huge, this fluctuation cannot remain for billions of years. Another important idea that Tryon came up with is that in fact there is no mass-energy in the universe. When scientists talk about mass-energy, they are overlooking an important form of energy, gravitational energy. Gravitation being an attractive force, gravitational energy is negative. What Tryon realized was that this negative form of energy exactly balanced positive form of energy, so that in effect total energy of the universe is zero. His brilliant idea has not however been developed in to a full-fledged cosmological model.

Another related idea is that of inflation. Inflation proposes that the universe entered a state of false vacuum soon after the Big Bang, and during that time universe expanded exponentially, much faster than observed Hubble rate, doubling in size every 10^{-34} second. During inflation positive form of mass-energy was created to balance the negative gravitational energy. In effect there was no creation of mass-energy. For this reason Alan Guth, who proposed inflation theory, considers the universe to be the ultimate free lunch. What Guth realized was there was no way to end the inflation period. A modification to inflation, called new inflation, is invoked to end the inflation, but this new theory is even more exotic. It proposes that there are many universes, one of which is our known. Inflation has not solved the singularity problem, as inflation only produces part of the mass-energy of the universe, and as long as even a tiny amount of mass-energy was present at time zero, singularity problem will be there. The Vedas tell us that at time zero there was no mass-energy in the universe. It was a complete void. Space, mass and energy are continuously being created. As universe had zero mass-energy at time equal to zero, the universe did not start with a singularity.

19.5: Conservation of space, matter and energy

In the beginning of this century, Einstein proved the equivalence of matter and energy. Today the Vedas have returned to tell an even greater truth: equivalence of space, matter and energy. Space is no different from matter and energy. In the beginning there was no mass-energy in the universe, because there was no space. Mass-energy is created due to expansion of the universe. Universe cannot expand without creating mass-energy, and universe cannot contract without annihilating mass-energy. Thus the universe started with zero mass-energy and will end up with zero mass-energy as well. There was no singularity in the beginning and there will be no singularity at the end. If this is the case, then mass-energy is being created right now as the universe is expanding. So should not scientists be witnessing this creation? In fact they are witnessing it right now, but have no clue as to what is it that they are observing. I am talking about gamma-ray bursts.

19.6: Gamma-ray bursts

Scientific American, July 97 has an article on gamma-ray bursts on page 46. The article begins by stating that about three times a day our sky flashes with a powerful pulse of gamma rays. The origin of these gamma-ray bursts is a complete mystery. These bursts were discovered in 1973 and several theories were floated to explain this phenomenon. Black holes, supernovae or neutron stars were thought to be the sources of these bursts. The most accepted theory is that of binary neutron stars collapsing, but there are problems with this explanation. The gamma-ray bursts are intense, bulk of their radiation is in the range 100,000 to 1,000,000 electron volts implying a very hot source and its sources release more energy within minutes than sun will release in its entire lifetime. Astronomers believe that these bursts are coming from cosmological distances probably three to ten billion light years away. The sources of these bursts are distributed isotropically, that is their number is same in any direction. The question is why? Are we in the center of a large spherical shell over which the sources of these bursts are uniformly distributed? The idea of us being in the center of this shell is unnerving to the scientists, because center is a special position and science does not allow for us to be in a special position compared to any other point in the universe.

We have seen that Vedic scientists consider the creation of mass-energy to be taking place continuously at the surface of the universe. We have also seen that the creation of mass-energy is related to the expansion of space. As the universe is huge now, its expansion will create immense radiation. As surface of the universe envelopes us from all direction, and this surface is far away from us, the gamma ray bursts will seem isotropic and seem to come from outer reaches of the universe. What is most significant is that these gamma-ray bursts are taking place three times a day, and this is exactly the frequency at which the creation of mass-energy is taking place according to the Vedic scientists. Here are some verses from the Ṛgveda to this effect:

"O Savitā, give us wealth every day three times a day." Ṛgveda 3.56.6

"O Agni, we know you have wealth to give three times a day to mortals." Ṛgveda 7.11.3

"O Soma, give us three times a day, what you have milked." Ṛgveda 9.86.18

There is a concept called "Digdāha" related to this creation at the surface of universe. Digdāha means fire at the boundaries, and refers to immense radiation being generated at the ends of the universe. This creation of mass-energy and space is called Yajña. Havana is performed three times a day because creation takes place three times a day. Without Yajña there would be no universe, and it is for this reason that Yajña is given so much importance in the Vedas. In Brāhmaṇas Viṣṇu is equated to Yajña again and again (Śatpatha Brāhmaṇa 1.1.2.13, 5.2.3.6, 5.4.5.1, Aitareya Brāhmaṇa 1.3.4, Kauṣītaki Brāhmaṇa 4.2, 1.8, 18.14). The reason being as universe (Viṣṇu) expands creation of mass-energy and space (Yajña) takes place. Yajña is also called Vitāna meaning expanding, because Yajña is related to the expansion of the the universe. Following question is asked in the Vedas:

"I ask you the remotest end of earth. I ask you what the origin of universe is." Ṛgveda 1.164.34, Yajurveda 23.61

And the answer is given as,

"This altar is the remotest end of earth. This Yajña is the origin of universe." Ṛgveda 1.164.35, Yajurveda 23.62

The remotest end of observer space is the boundary of the universe, and that is where the creation is taking place, therefore this boundary is considered the altar. Now we are in a position to piece together the evolution of the universe according to the Vedas.

19.7: Evolution of the universe

Before the creation, there existed an ultimate reality beyond our conceptions of space, matter and time. The ultimate reality desired to create the universe. With this desire, the universe started as a small fluctuation creating a tiny region of space with a very small amount of mass-energy. In the beginning there was neither space nor mass-energy. The universe did not start with a Big Bang. There was no mass-energy available to create this Big Bang. When I talk about the creation of mass-energy, it implies that it is accompanied by an equal amount of negative energy due to gravitation or other attractive forces. In effect, there is no creation and the total mass-energy is always zero. Initially the forces of attraction and repulsion were in a very delicate balance. First fluctuation was not very successful, and universe began to contract after an initial expansion. This contracting universe was called "Mārtaṇḍa". The forces of attraction and repulsion were then fine tuned and the universe started to expand again. This living universe was given the name "Vivasvāna". Space and mass-energy are closely related. When the universe became of a certain size, there became sufficient energy available for the formation of first pair of particle and its anti-particle. This first pair was given the name "Yama" or "Manu". With further expansion of the universe mass-energy of universe kept increasing with the formation of more pairs of particles and anti-particles. Somewhere along the line universe separated in three spaces, observer, intermediate and light. The electric force was the major force causing the expansion of the universe. In the early universe surface tension of the universe was the most important force constraining the expansion of the universe. The battle of these two forces was immortalized in the epic battle of Indra and Vṛtra. The particles and anti-particles annihilated each other changing in radiation. This radiation was called Rudra. The radiation gave rise to radiation pressure, which pushed universe to expand. Radiation pressure was given the name Maruta, and its components were described as sons of Rudra. As the universe was expanding, it started to rotate as well. This rotation gave rise to parity violation resulting in the production of a small excess of matter over antimatter. This small excess of matter accumulated over the age of the universe making the universe matter dominated. The annihilation of anti-matter was represented as the slaying of dark people by Indra. The remnants of radiation from early universe is observed as cosmic background radiation, which was named Viṣa.

As the universe started with zero matter and energy, the universe must have started cold, very cold. As the universe started to rotate, the shape of the universe changed to a spheroid or an egg. With the increase in mass-energy content, the gravitational pull also increased, which acted to slow down the expansion of the universe. The expansion rate and rotational velocity of the university have been constantly changing during the evolution of the universe as the strengths of the forces of expansion and contraction have kept changing. The universe started with zero expansion and rotational velocity, reached to a maximum, and then slowed down. We are currently somewhere in the later phase of the expansion, when the expansion velocity and rotational velocity both are very low. As the universe is a spheroid, it has a center and an axis of rotation. The universe has an eccentricity, which is changing with time. Halfway through the evolution of the universe, forces of expansion and contraction will come to an exact balance, bringing the universe to a complete halt, both expansion and rotational velocity becoming zero. Universe at this point will become a perfect sphere. The latter half of the evolution will then begin with the contraction of the universe and probably rotation of the universe in opposite direction. During this phase mass-energy of the universe will be gradually reduced. Finally universe will end where it began its journey with zero space, matter and energy.

19.8: Trinity

In Hinduism Brahmā, Viṣṇu and Maheśa form a trinity. Brahmā is the creator of the universe, Viṣṇu the protector and Maheśa the destroyer. Brahmā means expansion, and expansion of the universe takes place with the creation of matter and energy, thus Brahmā is creator. Viṣṇu is the life-principle of the universe, who is not different from the universe, thus he is the protector. Maheśa or Mahādeva or Śiva is Vedic god Rudra representing radiation. As radiation is the result of annihilation of particles, he is related to destruction. But what is annihilated is born again as another set of particles, and this dance of creation and annihilation continues. This is the cosmic dance of Śiva, and therefore he is called Naṭarāja, Lord of the dancers. With the Vedic framework in mind, we are in a position to solve the problems plaguing the Big Bang Model.

19.9: The horizon problem

The horizon problem is related to causal connectivity. How did the regions in space not causally connected get homogenized? If the universe started with a Big Bang, it should be chaotic and inhomogeneous. Inflation is used to provide a smoothening effect in big bang model, but it cannot be accepted as a proof, unless it is proved that inflation ever took place. Otherwise it can only be thought of as an ingenious device designed to hide the fatal flaws of the Big Bang Model.

The Vedic model tells us that the expansion of the universe started smoothly and has been smooth ever since. The universe didn't start with an explosion. The expansion was very slow in the beginning. Thus all parts of the universe were in equilibrium in the beginning, and the expansion has been smooth ever since. Thus two parts of the universe, which are not causally connected today, were causally connected in the beginning for a long time, and it is no wonder that the universe looks so smooth.

19.10: The flatness problem

The ratio of kinetic to gravitational energy in the universe is called omega. The measured value of omega is close to one. As the universe is between 10-20 billion years old in big-bang model, the omega at big bang must have been very close to one, up to 59 decimal points. If omega were even slightly greater than or less than one, by now omega would be either close to zero or infinity. Why was omega so close to one at Big Bang? Stated in another way, why are the kinetic and gravitational energy in such a delicate balance? One possible explanation is the unverifiable Inflation. The Vedic model provides an elegant solution to the flatness problem.

The total energy of the universe is equal to zero. The total energy of the universe can be divided in positive energy and negative energy. Positive and negative energies balance each other. Forms of positive energy are mass-energy, kinetic energy and rotational energy, while forms of negative energy are gravitational energy and surface energy. At time zero, all forms of energy had zero value, and their values have changed during the course of evolution subject to the condition that total energy must be zero at all times. Thus gravitational energy and kinetic energy will always remain in near balance. Kinetic energy and gravitational energy are not exactly equal though, because there are other forms of energy. In the beginning there was neither kinetic energy nor gravitational energy. As kinetic energy increased so did the gravitational energy. Net energy of the universe remains zero all the time, and thus omega always remains close to one.

19.11: The age problem

The age of the universe lies between 7 and 20 billion years depending on the value of Hubble constant and other factors. The value of Hubble constant itself is a matter of raging controversy. The age of oldest stars is between 13 and 17 billion years. The age of the elements is between 12 to 16 years. This brings a peculiar situation that universe may be younger than its constituents. Physicists favor the lowest value of Hubble constant to avoid the age problem.

In the Vedic model, the universe began with zero space volume, zero mass-energy and zero Hubble velocity. With the creation of matter-antimatter and their annihilation the Hubble velocity increased gradually. As space expanded further the gravitational pull of mass-energy started to slow down the expansion. Thus the Hubble velocity reached a maximum value, and then decreased slowly. In Vedic model, a condition like that of the Big Bang emerges when Hubble velocity reaches a maximum. However, by this time universe is considerably old. In the standard Big Bang model, probably more than half of the age of the universe is not even being looked into. Once the first half of the expansion is taken into account, the age of the universe may more than double. This may solve the age problem.

19.12: The monopole problem

Grand unified theory in conjunction with the big bang model predicts the existence of magnetic monopoles. The mass of the monopole should be approximately ten million billion billion times that of the proton. New inflation theory predicts that there are many universes like several bubbles, and each universe contains one monopole. Again, predictions of inflation cannot be tested. No monopoles have been found.

In the Vedic model the monopoles do not exist. The universe was immensely dense in the beginning giving rise to monopoles in the Big Bang model. As universes did not possess such high density in the Vedic model, the monopoles cannot be formed.

19.13: The entropy problem

Entropy is the measure of disorder in a system. According to Penrose, the entropy in the early universe was extremely low. Universe began as an extremely ordered system. This is in direct contradiction with the Big Bang model.

In the Vedic model, the entropy problem is solved, as universe began with zero entropy. There was no matter and energy at time equal to zero, so entropy was zero as well. Since the mass-energy of the universe has increased slowly, the entropy has also increased slowly. Entropy will reach its maximum value halfway through the evolution of the universe, when its expansion comes to a halt. So far universe follows the second law of thermodynamics, which states that entropy of a closed system keeps on increasing. During second half of the evolution, the entropy will start to decrease and the universe will finally end up with zero entropy.

19.14: The antimatter problem

As matter and antimatter is created and annihilated in pair, in the standard Big Bang model there should be same amount of matter and antimatter in the universe. However, our universe seems to be matter-dominated. Where is the corresponding anti-matter? Are there other galaxies made of antimatter in far recesses of universe?

In the Vedic model, the universe is rotating. So there is a small excess of matter over antimatter due to the violation of symmetry. As matter and antimatter are continuously being created at the surface of the universe from the beginning of the universe with an excess creation of matter over antimatter, there is left over matter after annihilation of all the antimatter. This small excess of matter has accumulated over the age of the universe and our universe consists of matter only.

19.15: Implications of the Vedic model

The universe started with zero value of all properties: volume of the universe, Hubble velocity, rotational velocity of space, entropy, matter content, energy content, temperature etc. All properties are well behaved functions in the proposed model with no singularity at the beginning or the end. As space expands and rotates, matter and antimatter is created at the surface of the universe.

In Vedic model, there is a center of universe, which is at absolute rest. The center of the universe is called Hiraṇyagarbha, the Golden Womb, in Vedas. There is an axis of the universe passing through this center around which universe is rotating. This axis is represented in Hinduism as Śivaliṅga. Hindu devotees pour milk or water on Śivaliṅga, which represents the flow of matter and energy from the boundary of the universe towards the center of the universe. The Vedas tell us that we have a specific location in the universe. It is important to find out the center of the universe, the axis of rotation and our location in the universe. The model of the universe in the Vedas is illustrated in Figure 19.1. Space can be divided in two parts: manifested space and unmanifested space. Our universe is the manifested space, and it is expanding into unmanifested space creating matter and energy. The creation of matter and antimatter continues as long as the universe is expanding. As universe is expanding at present, new matter and antimatter is being created at the surface of the universe even now. This means that if we look in the direction of the center of the universe, we will find older matter, and if we look in the opposite direction we will find younger matter.

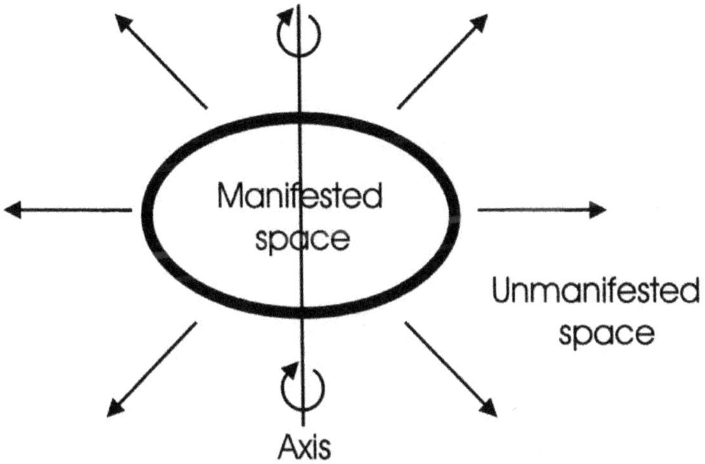

Figure 19.1: The Vedic model of the universe

Thus towards the center of the universe older galaxies will be seen, while in the opposite direction younger galaxies will be seen. The surface of the universe is in a violent state where matter and antimatter is being created continuously. It follows that we have a specific location in this universe. It will be highly improbable that we are at the center of the universe.

19.16: Cyclic cosmology

In the Big Bang model the universe can be either open or closed. The fate of the universe is decided by the balance of kinetic and potential energy. The fate of the universe is often compared with a projectile thrown from earth. If the projectile has sufficient velocity, it can escape from earth's gravitational pull. Otherwise it will reach a maximum height and then fall back on earth. In Vedic model a new twist is added to this analogy. Imagine a scenario in which the gravitational pull on the projectile increases as it goes further. In this case the projectile can never escape from earth's gravitational attraction. Similarly, the universe cannot keep expanding forever. The universe can only reach a maximum size and then collapse back on itself. The process of formation of the universe and its dissolution carries on according to the Vedas. The life of the universe in one cycle is called a "Kalpa". Cyclic nature of the universe is described in the famous "Aghamarṣaṇa" hymn of the Ṛgveda. Aghamarṣaṇa means "sin-effacing" and this hymn is recited daily by the Brāhmaṇas.

Ṛgveda 10.190

Sage: Mādhuchandasa Aghamarṣaṇa; Deity: Bhāvavṛtta;

Meter: Anuṣṭupa

1. Cosmic law and order were born from the inflaming heat. Then night was born and then foaming ocean.

2. From foaming ocean time was born. Night and day were made by the controller of the world like opening and closing of eye.

3. Founder created sun and moon **as earlier**, heaven and earth, atmosphere and Svaḥ as well.

Lord Kṛṣṇa says to Arjuna in Gītā, the epitome of Hindu philosophy:

"O son of Kuntī! All beings return to my nature at the end of Kalpa, and I create them again in the beginning of Kalpa." Gītā 9.7

"I control nature and create all these beings dependent on nature again and again." Gītā 9.8

Modern scientists have also considered the possibility of universe expanding and contracting again and again. Cyclic cosmology assumes that universe is closed and collapses back on itself and the cycle is repeated. It has been calculated that starlight will accumulate from cycle to cycle and it will cause each cycle to be longer than the earlier cycle. There cannot be more than 100 cycles according to these calculations. Some researchers have even looked for matter/radiation from earlier cycle.

According to the Vedic model these views about cyclic universe need to be modified. When the universe collapses back, it has zero mass-energy. A universe of zero space volume cannot have any mass-energy, because it cannot have any negative potential to balance the mass-energy. Thus there is no starlight accumulation, and there cannot be any matter/radiation from earlier cycle in our universe. Each cycle is completely independent, and thus there is no limitation on how many cycles there can be. There is no way to know about earlier cycle, as no information can travel from one cycle to another.

19.17: Vedic model and other cosmologies

Like Big Bang model, the Vedic model assumes that the universe has started from a point and is expanding. However, unlike the Big Bang model universe starts cold with zero mass-energy, and is rotating as well as expanding. The universe has a center, an axis of rotation and a non-spherical shape. There is a similarity with the Steady State model that mass-energy is constantly being created. The difference is that universe is not considered infinitely old, and the creation of mass-energy is only during the expansion phase of the universe. During the contraction phase, the mass-energy is annihilated, so that universe ends without a singularity. Table 19.1 shows the comparison between Vedic and modern cosmologies.

Table 19.1: A comparison of Vedic and modern cosmologies

Big Bang Cosmology	Steady State Cosmology	Vedic Cosmology
Universe had a beginning	Universe had no beginning	Universe had a beginning
Universe is not rotating	Universe is not rotating	Universe is rotating
Universe has no center	Universe has no center	Universe has a center
Universe is a spherical surface	Universe has no shape	Universe is a spheroid
Universe has no axis	Universe has no axis	Universe has an axis
Universe has no boundary	Universe has no boundary	Universe has a boundary
All the mass-energy was created in the beginning	There was no beginning	Mass-energy content was zero in the beginning
There is no creation of mass-energy now	Mass-energy is continuously being created	Mass-energy is continuously being created
There is no creation of mass energy taking place	Mass-energy is created everywhere in the universe	Mass-energy is created at the surface of the universe
There is no creation of mass-energy	Creation takes place in the form of hydrogen atom	Creation takes place in the form of matter and anti-matter
Universe started very hot	Universe was always same	Universe started very cold

"My suspicion is that the universe is not only queerer than we suppose, but queerer than we can suppose."
- J. B. S. Haldane

20. THE ASTRONOMICAL CODE

Professor Subhash Kak is an eminent scientist, philosopher, and Indologist. He has demonstrated that the Brāhmī script is derived from the earlier Indus-Saraswatī script. In his book "The Astronomical Code of the Ṛgveda" Professor Kak has described the astronomical information in the arrangement of Vedic verses, which will be briefly described in this chapter [1]. I will remind my readers that this astronomical information is coded in the lay-out of the verses, and it is my opinion that there is no astronomical information in the meaning of the verses. The subject matter of the Ṛgveda is cosmology, and not astronomy. The interpretation of the verses for astronomical dating of Vedas, for example by Jacobi and Tilak, is entirely unsatisfactory. I should also stress that What Professor Kak has discovered may only be the tip of the iceberg. The Vedas might be carrying much more scientific information in their arrangement, if the mind-boggling physics of the Vedas is any indication.

The Ṛgveda is divided in two ways. Most commonly, the Ṛgveda is divided in ten books called Maṇḍalas. Each maṇḍala is further divided in hymns called Sūktas and each Sūkta contains several verses called Ṛchās. Each Ṛchā is set to a metre called Chhandas. There are seven prominent Chhandas. Each Chhanda has a set number of pādas, and pādas have a set number of syllables.The most popular Chhanda is Gāyatrī, which consists of three pādas, each of eight syllables, thus the Gāyatrī Chhanda consists of twenty four syllables. Śatapatha Brāhmaṇa 10.4.2.23-24 describes the Ṛgveda as having 432,000 syllables, but actual count is much less, only 394,317. The huge gap is irreconcilable, because Vedas have been extremely well preserved. The authors of the Śatapatha Brāhmaṇa have simply assumed the number of syllables in order to give additional meaning to the Vedas, again a sign of loss of the Vedic science.

Ten books of the Ṛgveda contain following number of hymns: 191, 43, 62, 58, 87, 75, 104, 92, 114 and 191 consecutively. First and last books are ascribed to a number of sages, while books two to eight are considered family books, each book containing hymns by a prominent sage and his family members. We have met these sages in a previous chapter. Book nine is also ascribed to a number of sages, but the deity of all hymns in this book is Soma, while rest of the books contains hymns dedicated to a large number of deities. Total number of hymns in Ṛgveda is 1017. There are eleven additional hymns in the Ṛgveda called Vālakhilya hymns, which are found in the eighth book from hymns 49 to 59. Vālakhilya hymns consist of eighty verses. Total number of verses in the Ṛgveda is 10,442 without counting Vālakhilya hymns.

The Ṛgveda is also divided in eight parts called Aṣṭaka, each further subdivided in eight sub-parts called Adhyāya. Thus Ṛgveda contains sixty four adhyāyas. Adhyāyas are further divided in Vargas. There are 2006 Vargas in Ṛgveda. There are varying numbers of verses in each Varga.

Total number of hymns in the Ṛgveda is 1017. The Ṛgveda considers universe to be divided in three spaces, thus there are 339 verses per space. What is the significance of number 339? Number 339 is related to another sacred Hindu number 108. Hindus recite sacred mantras 108 times. The average distance of the sun from the earth is approximately 108 times the diameter of the sun and the average distance of moon from earth is approximately 108 times the diameter of the moon. It is for this remarkable coincidence that the sun and the moon seem to be of same size as viewed from earth. Number 339 is approximately π times number 108. This represents the number of disks of sun or moon to cover their paths across sky. The sum of number of hymns in books 1 and 10 is 382. The sum of number of hymns in books 2, 3, 5 and 7 is 296. Number 339 is the average of 296 and 382, and also the sum of number of hymns in books 4, 6, 8 and 9. Number 339 is 43 less than number 382 and 43 greater than 296. Numbers 296, 339 and 382 are the number of sun-steps during the winter solstice, equinox and summer solstice respectively. Ratio of 382 to 296 is 1.29 and represents the ratio of the duration of the longest to the shortest day where composition of the Vedas took place.

The arrangement of hymns in the Vedas contains information about the sidereal and synodic periods of the planets Mercury, Venus, Mars, Jupiter and Saturn. Table 20.1 shows the the astronomical information about the synodic periods of the planets.

The probability of these numbers showing up at random is very small, and proves that the Vedic sages knew the planetary periods well and incorporated that knowledge in the arrangement of the Vedas. I hope that one day we will understand the meaning of the Vedas completely and appreciate our invaluable Vedic heritage.

Table 20.1: The structure of the Ṛgveda and the synodic period of the planets

Planet	Synodic Period	Hymn combinations
Mercury	115.88	118 = Books (2+6)
Venus	583.92	583 = Books (1+5+9+10)
Mars	779.94	779 = Books (1+5+7+8+9+10)
Jupiter	398.88	398 = Books (2+3+5+8+9)
Saturn	378.09	377 = Books (2+4+5+6+9)

SCIENTIFIC GLOSSARY

Vedic term	Apparent meaning	Scientific meaning
Agni	Fire	Energy
Aja	Goat	Localized energy
Antarikṣa	Atmosphere	Intermediate space
Āpaḥ	Water	Matter-antimatter
Āraṇya	Wild animal	Fermion
Aryamā	God Aryamā	Neutron
Aśva	Horse	Aśva particle
Aśvin	Twin gods	Magnetic poles
Avi	Sheep	Avi particle
Bṛhaspati	God Bṛhaspati	Expansion of the universe
Chakra	Wheel	Rotation of universe
Dyau	Heaven	Light space
Gau	Cow	Gau particle
Grāmya	Domesticated animal	Boson
Hiraṇya	Gold	Color of energy
Indra	God Indra	Electric force
Indu	Soma juice	Electricity
Madhu	Honey	Magnetic field
Maruta	Wind	Radiation pressure
Mitra	God Mitra	Proton
Nakta	Night	Annihilation of particles
Pṛthivī	Earth	Observer space
Puṣā	God Puṣā	Set of particles
Rudra	God Rudra	Radiation

Vedic term	Apparent meaning	Scientific meaning
Salila	Water	Primordial fluid
Savitā	God Savitā	Creation-annihilation Energy
Soma	Soma plant	Electric charge
Sūrya	Sun	Light
Uṣā	Dawn	Creation of particles
Varuṇa	God Varuṇa	Electron
Vasiṣṭha	Sage Vasiṣṭha	Nucleus
Vāyavya	Bird	Field particle
Vāyu	Air	Field
Viṣṇu	God Viṣṇu	Universe
Vṛtra	Demon Vṛtra	Surface tension

NOTES

Chapter 1: The Vedic Legacy

1. Mīmāṃsaka (1976): 40
2. Sātavalekar (1993)
3. Rāmagopāla (1985)
4. Vidyālaṅkāra (1976)
5. Pāṇḍeya (1994)
6. Upretī (1985)
7. Vedālaṅkāra (1981)
8. Rajaram (1993): 19, 20
9. Das (1921)

Chapter 2: The Time before Time

1. Lang (1995): 190
2. Catlin (1996)
3. Lang (1995): 201

Chapter 3: All This is Puruṣa

1. Lang (1995): 185

Chapter 5: Edge of the Universe

1. Lang (1995): 42, 43
2. Parpola (1994): 91

Chapter 6: Parallel spaces

1. Guggenheim (1952): 166

Chapter 9: Quark Confinement

1. Horgan (1996)

Chapter 10: Matter and Energy

1. Ne'eman and Kirsh (1996): 198

Chapter 11: Electron, Proton and Neutron
1. Ne'eman and Kirsh (1996): 78
2. Ulansey (1989): 36
3. Ulansey (1989): 118
4. Cumont (1956): 190, 191
5. Cumont (1956): 201

Chapter 13: Let There Be Light
1. Rao and Kak (1998): 80

Chapter 14: The Dance of Creation
1. Tilak (1925)

Chapter 18: Did Big Bang Happen?
1. Misner, Thorne and Wheeler (1973): 704
2. Parker (1993): 159-176, 259-279

Chapter 19: The Vedic Cosmology
1. Nodland and Ralston (1997)

Chapter 20: The Astronomical code
1. Kak (1994)

BIBLIOGRAPHY

Catlin, G. 1996. *Life among the Indians*. London, UK: Bracken Books.

Cumont, F. 1956. *The Mysteries of Mithra*. New York, USA: Dover Publications.

Das, A. C. 1921. *Ṛgvedic India*. Bengal, India: University of Calcutta Press.

Guggenheim, E.A. 1952. *Mixtures*. Oxford, UK: Oxford University Press.

Horgan, J. 1996. *The End of Science*. Boston, Massachusetts, USA: Addison Wesley.

Kak, S. 1994. *The Astronomical Code of the Ṛgveda*. New Delhi, India: Aditya Prakashan.

Lang, A. 1995. *Myth, Ritual and Religion,Volume One*. London, UK: Senate.

Mīmāṃsaka, Y. 1976. *Vaidika Siddhanta Mīmāṃsā*. Sonipat, Haryana, India: Yudhiṣṭhira Mīmāṃsaka Publication.

Misner, C.W., Thorne, K.S., and Wheeler, J.A. 1973. *Gravitation*. San Francisco, USA: W. H. Freeman and Company.

Ne'eman, Y. and Kirsh, Y. 1996. *Particle Hunters*. Cambridge, UK: Cambridge University Press.

Nodland, B. and Ralston, J.P. 1997. *Physical Review Letters*, 78 (16), April 21.

Pāṇḍeya, S. 1994. *Bṛhaspati Sūkton Kā Ālochanātmaka Adhyayana*. Delhi, India: Pratibhā Prakāśana.

Parker, B. 1993. *The Vindication of the Big Bang*. New York, USA: Plenum Press.

Parpola, A. 1994. *Deciphering the Indus script*, Cambridge, UK: Cambridge University Press.

Rajaram, N.S. 1993. *Aryan Invasion of India, The Myth and the Truth*. New Delhi, India: Voice of India.

Rāmagopāla. 1985. *Vedārtha Vimarśa*. Chandigarh, India: Punjab University.

Rao, T.R.N. and Kak, S. (ed.). 1998. *Computing Science in Ancient India*. Lafayette, Louisiana: University of Southwestern Louisiana.

Sātavalekar, S.D. 1993. *Ṛgveda Kā Subodha Bhāṣya*, Four volumes. Killa-Pardi, Gujarat, India: Swādhyāya Maṇḍala.

Tilak, B. G. 1925. *The Arctic home in the Vedas*. Pune, Maharashtra, India: Pūnā Tilak Bros.

Ulansey, D. 1989. *The Origins of the Mithraic Mysteries*. New York, USA: Oxford University Press.

Upretī, J. 1985. *Veda Meṃ Indra*. Delhi, India: Bhāratīya Vidyā Prakāśana.

Vedālaṅkāra, B. 1981. *Savitā Devatā*. Delhi, India: Śrī Saraswatī Sadana.

Vidyālaṅkāra, R. 1976. *Vedoṃ Kī Varṇana Śailiyān*, Haridwar, Uttarakhand, India: Gurukul Kangri Press.

INDEX

Aditi, 47, 48, 53, 75, 76, 78, 142, 161
Āditya, 13, 48, 85, 106, 116, 124, 142, 147, 160, 192, 216
Agastya, 54-56, 78, 186-188
Age problem, 205, 222
Agni, 36, 51, 64, 65, 77, 81, 85, 97-99, 106, 110, 112, 121, 122, 124, 126, 128, 138, 142, 153, 160, 161, 163, 184, 192, 217
Ahi, 13-15
Ahuramazdā, 140, 141
Aja, 114, 115, 118, 122, 123, 127, 132, 170
Ajāśva, 132
Animal sacrifice, 41, 119, 120, 125
Antarikṣa, 37, 58, 71-73, 77, 81, 83, 84, 89, 93, 106, 148
Antimatter problem, 207, 223
Āpaḥ, 24, 25, 42, 46, 64, 97-99, 124, 176, 187
Apollo, 69, 93
Apsarā, 185-187
Āptya, 93, 121
Āraṇya, 35, 36, 113, 121
Arjuna, 227
Aryamā, 4, 130, 138, 146, 147
Aśva, 83, 114-118, 122, 132, 150
Atri, 190
Aurobindo, 19
Avi, 114-116, 122, 123, 150, 170

Bala, 50, 65, 66, 110
Balarāma, 194, 195
Bali, 75
Baryon, 119, 120
Bhaga, 166
Bharadwāja, 190
Bharata, 7, 185
Bhāratī, 106-108
Big Bang, 35, 46, 55, 57, 63, 64, 95, 197, 199-207, 211-228
Bondi, Hermann, 202
Boson, 113, 119, 120

Brahma, 32, 45, 50, 205
Brahmā, 74, 100, 220
Brahmaṇaspati, 47, 50-52
Brahmāṇḍa 45, 73
Bṛhaspati, 47, 50, 53, 64, 126, 180, 181

Capra, Fritjof, 165
Chokanipok, 42
Cletor, 43
Copernicus, 45, 199
Cosmic egg, 209
Cosmic tree, 86
Cumont, Franz, 145, 146
Cyclic cosmology, 226, 227

Dakṣa, 47, 53, 168
Dalton, John, 119
Dānu, 59, 66
Dark matter, 95, 203
Darwin, 195
Das, A.C., 17
Dayānanda, 19
Deluge, 16, 25, 26
Dicke, 204
Digdāha, 217
Dvaipāyana, Kṛṣṇa, 8
Dvita, 121
Dyau, 37, 71-73, 76-78, 81, 82, 84, 85, 88, 93, 97, 106, 148
Dyāvāpṛthivī, 72, 78, 85

Einstein, 45, 113, 191, 200, 215
Ekata, 121
Electron, 2, 118-120, 135, 137, 139, 140, 141, 146, 148, 161, 177, 178, 187, 188, 213
Eliot, T.S., 209
Entropy problem, 206, 223
Erinnys, Demeter, 83

Fermion, 113, 119
Feynman, Richard, 199
Flatness problem, 204, 205, 221

Gaia, 86
Gamma-ray bursts, 215, 216
Gandharva, 116, 176
Gaṇeśa, 193
Gaṅgā, 100, 133
Garuḍa, 145
Gates, Sylvester James, 91, 127
Gau, 13-15, 114-116, 122, 124-126, 150, 153, 162
Gauge boson, 119, 120
Gautama, 190
Gāyatrī, 108, 128, 131, 142, 147, 151, 232
Gell-Mann, M., 120, 131
Giant tortoise, 88, 89
Gibbs, 72
Gold, Thomas, 202
Golden womb, 21, 77, 224

Gotra, 67
Grāmya, 35, 36, 113-115, 118-125
Guggenheim, 72
Guth, Alan, 214

Hadron, 120
Haldane, J.B.S., 231
Hariśchandra, 178
Heisenberg, 111, 173
Hera, 83
Hercules, 68
Horizon problem, 203, 204, 220
Hoyle, Fred, 202
Hubble, Edwin, 57, 63, 200, 205, 214, 222, 224

Ilā, 106-108
Indra, 13-15, 34, 36, 50, 51, 56-69, 74, 76, 93, 97-110, 116, 117, 121, 122, 124, 126, 130, 134, 149-154, 163, 175, 178-182, 184-187, 192, 193, 218, 219
Indu, 151, 152
Ioskeha, 60

Jacobi, 17, 231
Jaimini, 8

Kak, Subhash, 162, 231
Kālī, 137
Kalpa, 226, 227
Kaṇva, 190
Kaśyapa, 48, 75, 100
Kātyāyana, 192
Kautsa, 18
Kepler, 199
Kośa, 74
Kṛṣṇa, 17, 137, 194, 195, 227

Lakṣmī, 53
Lee, Tsung-Dao, 211
Leontocephalous Kronos, 144
Lepton, 119-121
Loka, 37, 38, 58, 71, 72, 81, 90, 100
Lopāmudrā, 54-56

Madhu, 152-155
Mahābhārata, 7-10, 20, 29, 43, 48, 75, 89, 144, 194
Mahādeva, 220
Mahākāla, 196
Mahāpralaya, 32, 46
Maheśa, 74, 220
Mahīdhara, 4, 19, 72
Manu, 25, 26, 48, 218
Marshall, 38
Mārtaṇḍa, 47, 48, 218
Martyaloka, 81
Maruta, 31, 101-108, 112, 219
Māyā, 73, 139
Māyājāla, 73
Medusa, 69
Meson, 119, 120

Mīmāṃsaka, Yudhiṣṭhira, 7
Misner, 203
Mithra, 143-146
Mitra, 4, 13, 106, 128, 130, 138, 140-143, 146, 147, 152, 160, 161, 176, 186-188
Monopole problem, 206, 222
Müler, Max, 16, 17, 19, 107

Nakta, 165, 168, 170
Nāsadīya hymn, 29
Naṭarāja, 171, 220
Ne'eman, Yuval, 131
Neutron, 119, 120, 135, 137, 146, 216
Newton, 113, 159, 200
Nodland, Borge, 212, 213
Nut, 86

Omorca, 42
Orion, 17
Osiris, 42
Ouranos, 86

Paila, 8
Pangu, 86
Paṇi, 51, 59, 179-182
Paradise, 42
Parama Vyoma, 27
Paraśurāma, 194
Parpola, Asko, 67
Paśu, 35, 112, 113, 120, 123
Pauli, Wolfgang, 211
Penrose, Roger, 206, 223
Persephone, 43
Perseus, 69
Photon, 114, 120, 162, 168
Prajāpati, 10, 22, 30, 42, 43, 49, 61, 75, 112, 115, 192
Proto-Śiva, 133, 135
Proton, 118-120, 135, 137, 141- 143, 146, 161, 187, 206, 222
Pṛthivī, 37, 71-73, 77, 81, 84, 85, 88-90, 93, 97, 106, 199
Pura, 30, 34, 58, 186
Purandara, 34, 58
Pururavā, 106
Puruṣa, 29-43, 53, 58, 72, 88, 95, 105, 112, 115, 120, 125, 143, 144
Puruṣa hymn, 4, 28-30, 38, 41, 42, 44, 72, 113-115, 143
Pūṣā, 114, 130-135
Pytho, 69, 93

Quark, 111, 118, 120-122, 126

Ralston, John, P., 212, 213
Rāma, 194
Renan, Ernst, 137
Rodasī, 101
Rohita, 178, 179
Roth, 19
Rudra, 19, 67, 100-102, 105, 106, 124, 130, 192, 193, 218-220

Russell, Bertrand, 183

Śākala, 4
Śakti, 53, 193
Salila, 22, 24, 25, 42, 46, 47, 98, 99, 113, 210
Śambara, 50, 66
Śambhu, 101
Śaṅkara, 101
Śaṅkarāchārya, 29
Saramā, 179-182
Saraṇyū, 82, 83
Saraswatī, 49, 105-110
Sātavalekara, 15, 19, 168
Śaunaka, 4, 50, 65, 188
Savitā, 13, 14, 127-130, 132, 135, 155, 156, 166, 170, 216
Sāyaṇa, 19, 31, 72, 106-108, 162, 163
Schrödinger, Erwin, 71
Seb, 86
Śeṣanāga, 69, 88, 145
Shaw, George Bernard, 45
Singularity problem, 203, 215
Śiva, 53, 69, 100, 101, 133, 135, 165, 171, 184, 193, 196, 220
Śivaliṅga, 224
Smṛti, 2
Soma, 31, 55, 56, 58, 59, 64-66, 99, 103, 109, 114-116, 125, 131, 138, 149-152, 155, 163, 180, 181, 185-187, 217, 232
Śruti, 2
Steady State, 202, 207, 228
Sudāsa, 185, 187
Śukrāchārya, 100
Sumantu, 8
Śunaḥ Śepa, 178, 179
Superspace, 90, 91
Sūrya, 14, 76, 77, 98, 100, 104, 124, 130, 159-163, 166, 168, 192, 193

Tapa, 23-24
Thomson, J.J., 119
Tilak, 17, 167, 231
Toynbee, Arnold, 145
Triśirā Viśvarūpa, 93, 94
Trita, 15, 62, 63, 93, 116, 118, 121, 126
Triton, 118
Tṛtsu, 185, 186
Tryon, Ed, 214
Tvaṣṭā, 58, 82, 93, 176

Unicorn, 38, 41, 120
Uranus, 86
Urvaśī, 187
Uṣā, 66, 160, 163, 165-171, 185
Uvvaṭa, 19

Vaiśampāyana, 5, 8
Vāk, 105-107

Varāha, 62, 63, 76, 138, 194
Varuṇa, 4, 13, 64, 67, 99, 106, 116, 128, 130, 137-141, 143, 146, 147, 160, 161, 166, 176-179, 186-188
Vasiṣṭha, 4, 99, 184-189
Vāṣkali, 100
Vasu, 106, 116, 124, 192
Vasumanta, 50, 52
Vaucouleurs, Gerard de, 63
Vāyavya, 35, 36, 113, 121
Vāyu, 36, 46, 64, 71, 77, 83-85, 97, 98, 101, 104, 105, 113, 163, 192
Vedavyāsa, 8, 29
Verethraghna, 68
Vikramāditya, 195, 196
Viṣa, 219
Viṣṇu, 26, 46, 53, 62, 64, 67, 69, 74-76, 100, 144, 145, 163, 193, 194, 210, 217, 220
Viśwāmitra, 4, 110, 142, 184, 188, 190
Vīvaṅgahvanta, 48
Vivekānanda, 1
Vṛtra, 56-63, 67-69, 74, 88, 93, 102, 104, 109, 110, 138, 144, 148, 163, 182, 218
Vṛtrāghna, 68

Weinberg, Steven, 21, 97
Wu, Chien Shung, 211

Yajña, 7, 11, 34, 35, 37, 61, 75, 79, 113, 120, 147, 151, 152, 155-157, 192, 217
Yājñavalkya, 5
Yama, 48, 49, 82, 116, 129, 175-177, 185, 186, 218
Yamī, 82, 175-177
Yang, 86
Yang, Chen Ning, 211
Yāska, 18, 31
Yima, 49
Yin, 86
Ymir, 42

Zagreus, Dionysus, 42
Zeus, 43, 83
Zweig, George, 120
Zwicky, Fritz, 63

www.ingramcontent.com/pod-product-compliance
Lightning Source LLC
Chambersburg PA
CBHW061634040426
42446CB00010B/1417
* 9 7 8 1 9 8 8 2 0 7 0 4 9 *